"Brilliant and provocative, *Solo* transcends the loneliness narrative surrounding single life. It's not just about being okay with being alone; it's about the incredible freedom and endless opportunities that come with it. McGraw combines science and wisdom to unlock the secrets that Solos have always known: life is richer when you're the hero of your own story."

—KRISTIN NEWMAN,
author of *What I was Doing While You Were Breeding*

"With the country's focus on finding a soulmate, Peter allows unmarrieds to embrace living an authentic life of personal growth without being in a traditional relationship. The book (and the movement) is a refreshing look at how one can thrive being solo and explore ways to redefine and repurpose the old paradigm of sex, dating, and relationships."

—PAUL FARAHVAR,
host of *Singles Only!* Podcast

"*Solo* is a beautifully written book. Drawing from personal to academic sources, McGraw provides a much needed and timely roadmap for those that are single, those that know someone who is single, those recently returning to singlehood, those who want to be single, and even those who are no longer single."

—KRIS MARSH,
author of *The Love Jones Cohort*

"As a listener and fan of McGraw's *Solo* podcast, I was excited to hear that a book was finally in the works. And I expected nothing less than what was delivered in this funny, unique, insightful and important book. For too long, Solos have been sitting quietly on the sidelines whilst their coupled counterparts have taken up the field. No more. McGraw makes it abundantly clear that there is fun, freedom, and fulfilment to be had in taking the non-traditional path in life. Whether you're a Just May, a No Way, or a New Way, make no mistake that doing it Your Way can lead to a life full of joy and meaning."

—LUCY MEGGESON,
Host of *Spinsterhood Reimagined* Podcast

"In addition to being refreshingly optimistic about single life—making me feel seen and validating my choices—the advice in *Solo* for leading a remarkable life beautifully echoes what I shared in my book around healing from a serious illness. Nurturing friendships, the role that pets can play, fostering financial health, and leading a purpose-filled life are key to both. Additionally, we both highlighted the ways in which single people are the ones with the bandwidth to dedicate toward making the world a better place through significant acts of service and/or creating new organizations and movements. This book is a must-read for every "solo" on the planet!"

—TRACY MAXWELL,
author of *Being Single, With Cancer: A Solo Survivor's
Guide to Life, Love, Health and Happiness*

"This book would make a lousy wedding gift. But if you want to be single and happy, you're looking in the right place. Behavioral economist Peter McGraw draws on scientific research, personal narrative, and the stories of remarkable Solos to show how single people lead rich and fulfilling lives."

—WILLIAM VON HIPPEL,
award-winning author of *The Social Leap*

# SOLO

# SOLO

BUILDING A REMARKABLE

LIFE OF YOUR OWN

## PETER McGRAW

DIVERSION
BOOKS

NEW YORK

Diversion Books
A division of Diversion Publishing Corp.
www.diversionbooks.com

Diversion Books and colophon are registered trademarks of
Diversion Publishing Corp.

For more information, email info@diversionbooks.com.

First Diversion Books Edition: January 2024
Paperback ISBN 978-1-635-7688-62
e-ISBN 978-1-635-7693-33

Book Design by Aubrey Khan, Neuwirth & Associates, Inc.

Printed in the United States of America

1   2   3   4   5   6   7   8   9   10

Diversion books are available at special discounts for bulk purchases
in the US by corporations, institutions, and other organizations.
For more information, please contact admin@diversionbooks.com

To my single, divorced, separated, widowed, and married brothers and sisters, I dedicate this book to our shared experiences beyond our relationship status.

# CONTENTS

# BREAKING THE RULES IN A
# WORLD BUILT FOR TWO

'm Peter McGraw.

Twenty years ago, I celebrated my bachelor party. Fifteen friends visited my new home in the foothills of the Rocky Mountains to wish me hearty congratulations. I was a thirty-four year old behavioral scientist and new professor at the University of Colorado Boulder. It was Family Weekend at the university and hotel rooms were scarce, so I rented out my neighbors' apartments for a weekend of hiking, tailgating, poker, Wiffle ball, and the obligatory bar crawl. Speeches were given. Glasses clinked. Backs were slapped.

There was just one hitch.

I wasn't getting hitched.

With no fiancée or love interest to speak of, I threw myself a bachelor party.

Married people celebrate their relationship in numerous ways: engagement parties, wedding showers, rehearsal dinners, weddings, honeymoons, anniversaries, and, of course, bachelor parties. I thought, *Who made the rule that you need to marry to celebrate your singlehood?*

The invitation promised my friends they could "skip my real bachelor party—should I ever have one."

The attendees made the right choice. I never married. Never will.

At the time of the party, I had harbored doubts about matrimony for more than half my life. The question came up at my high school lunch table one day: "When will you get married?"

*When*, not if.

My pimply friends tasked with determining our destiny were in consensus: "Soon after college." Their answers were in line with the norms of the day. The average age of first marriage was twenty-five, our parents became parents by thirty, and the only bachelor I knew in my New Jersey neighborhood was George, a thirty-something neighbor who grew weed and drove a Trans Am.

I wanted to tell the table that we were getting way ahead of ourselves. "Rather than thinking about finding a wife, maybe you fools should try a little harder in home economics? Besides, none of us have even touched a boob." Instead, I chickened out and answered, "Not 'til after I'm thirty."

At sixteen, my less-than-enthusiastic response about marriage was justified given my less-than-stellar childhood. My parents failed to find the "happily ever after" promoted by the number one television show of the day: *The Cosby Show.* Dad was no Heathcliff; he was absent and struggling with alcoholism. Mom was far from Clair; she was angry and struggling to keep the lights on. They divorced when I was nine and my sister was seven.

With your friends, family members, and colleagues coupling up and settling down, you may sometimes feel like the only single person you know. An outcast. However, demographers are paying keen attention to the rise in the number of people staying single across the globe. One hundred twenty-seven million adults in the United States are single. That's nearly one in two adults. If singles are outcasts, they are the new in-group.

One reason for the rise is that people are marrying later. The average age of first marriage is creeping up toward thirty. (Maybe I wasn't the only one biting my tongue at the lunch table.) Thus, people who eventually partner up and settle down spend a greater proportion of their life single (figure 1). Data

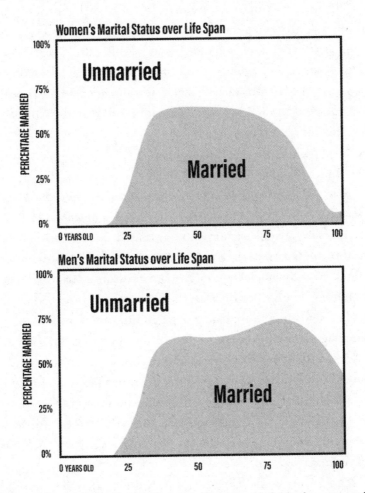

**FIGURE 1:** People spend most of their life unmarried (single, separated, divorced, or widowed). Women are more likely to be unmarried later in life, whereas men are more likely to be unmarried earlier in life. Figure adapted from Flowing Data (2016).

suggests that the average woman born today is expected to spend more of her life without a partner than married. Because marriage tends to sit in the middle of life, singleness is not evenly distributed across the life span. Young and old people are more likely to be single.

The patterns of singlehood also vary between men and women. More young men are single than women; however, this pattern flips as people get older. Gender differences in relationship status reflect men's shorter life expectancy, their tendency to marry later in life, and the fact that young men are unappealing to date. I know. I was one. No matter how good I got at laser tag, I couldn't impress the ladies.

Most people manage to couple up, but staying coupled is difficult. People like to throw around the statistic that 50 percent of marriages end in divorce. However, that stat divides the number of marriages by the number of divorces in the same year. That is not an apples-to-apples comparison. For example, if the number of marriages in a year went down, then the divorce rate would go up. That makes no sense, but if you are a fifty-something watching your friends divorce, the 50 percent statistic *feels* true.

The few longitudinal studies examining the time course of marriages reveal that about one in three contemporary marriages in the United States will end in divorce. Even for the two out of three people who avoid divorce, they face a 50 percent likelihood that their spouse will outlive them, and they will be single again. In all likelihood, the surviving spouse will be a woman, which explains why the spin-off *The Golden Guys* was never made.

The rise of single living is not only due to people spending less of their lives partnered. More people are choosing to be single *forever*. Of the one in two adults in the United States who are single, one in two of them are not interested in dating (figure 2). The trend is especially strong for younger people. Pew Research Center projections reveal that up to one in four millennials will never marry. (And the way things are going, the other three might marry each other.)

My favorite statistic of all? One hundred percent of all people were, are, or will again be single. As Mae West quipped, "I'm single because I was born that way."

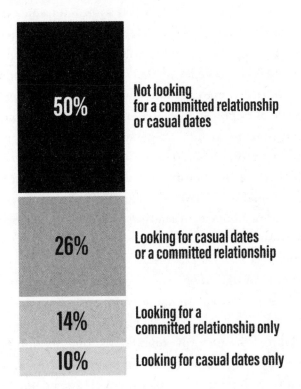

**50%** — Not looking for a committed relationship or casual dates

**26%** — Looking for casual dates or a committed relationship

**14%** — Looking for a committed relationship only

**10%** — Looking for casual dates only

**FIGURE 2:** Half of singles are not looking for a committed relationship or to casually date. Data from Pew Research Center (2020).

Besides being born single and staying single, people are living alone in unprecedented numbers. One-person households are the most common living arrangement in the United States, comprised of 28 percent of households. Two-person households make up the second most common type of living arrangement at 24.6 percent. The traditional nuclear family, defined as a married couple with children under eighteen years old, has fallen to third at 19.5 percent.

More and more people are recognizing that single living agrees with them—and provides freedom and flexibility to pursue remarkable opportunities. A Pew Research Center study in 2019 found that fewer people in the United States are seeing marriage as a necessary part of a fulfilling life, with less than 50 percent of US adults believing that society would be better off if people prioritized marriage and having children.

The rise of singles and living alone is a global phenomenon, with the percentage of one-person households increasing exponentially (figure 3). The number of one-person households is highest in Scandinavian countries: Norway (46 percent), Denmark (44 percent), Finland (43 percent), and Sweden (43 percent). Cities have even higher rates: Stockholm and London compete for number one and two in the world, respectively.

At the same time that I was skeptical about matrimony, I yearned for romance, companionship, and someone to sleep with. Not surprisingly, as a teenager, girls were as foreign to me as the lands I dreamed of someday visiting. My only shot at prom was with a girl who ended up taking her friend. I spent the evening with the guys eating Chinese food and watching an Arnold Schwarzenegger film. I waited another fifteen years to fall in love, get cheated on, and again find myself eating Chinese food and watching Arnold Schwarzenegger films.

As I started to have some romantic success, those relationships were often wonderful but ill-fitting—like wearing a badly

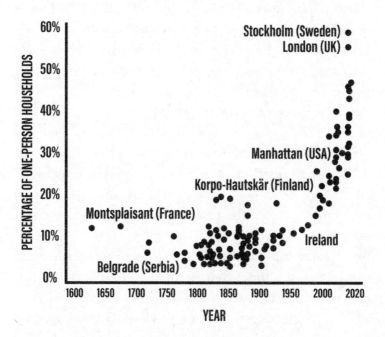

**FIGURE 3:** The number of adults living alone has nearly doubled in the past fifty years. This is a worldwide phenomenon that began more than one hundred years ago in industrialized countries, and is especially common in wealthier nations. Figure adapted from Our World in Data (2019).

tailored $3,000 suit. A relationship model where your romantic partner had to be your *everything* felt more like a straitjacket to me.

WHEN I WAS IN A STRAITJACKET—err, I mean long-term relationship—about a year and half in (if we made it that far), my girlfriend would want to move in. Knowing the implications of my answer, I would reluctantly say no, we would cry, and the relationship would end.

Another issue that made partnering difficult is that I never wanted children. Some of it was a practical matter; I had too many other things I wanted to do. Some of it was a feeling that children would not make me happy. After all, being parents didn't make my parents happy. Quite the opposite.

Ends up, I am a trendsetter. Data from the Pew Research Center in 2020 reveals a decrease in US fertility rates, dropping to just 1.73 births over a women's lifetime in 2018. This figure lies notably beneath the required replacement level of 2.1 births. The drop in people having children, which has been happening steadily since 1960, further diminishes the perceived need to get married.

In my late thirties, a chance meeting on a business trip led to a romance with a funny, introverted fashionista. Despite my stance that "long distance is the wrong distance," we began a passionate love affair. She made me feel like the most important person in the world. The relationship was intoxicating but still ill-fitting. The fashionista, who was in her mid-thirties and wanted children, had no time to waste on a man who was more interested in a vasectomy than a family vacation.

The relationship came to an end. Cue the crying. We are still friends, and she got her wish: a big house in the suburbs, two kids, and a designer lapdog. I suspect the breakup saved us from a divorce and custody battle for the dog.

That said, the breakup was agonizing. I was a mess for a full year. Chinese food, Arnold Schwarzenegger films, the works. I wanted this wonderful woman in my life, but to do so, I would need to change what I wanted from my life. As I grieved and wondered what was wrong with me for failing to make *another* relationship work, I had an insight that may seem mundane, but was profound to me. I remember exactly where I was standing in my apartment when it hit me:

**"I am happy when I am single."**

It was a eureka moment, but the insight had been simmering for some time. Sure, I had problems, but on balance, I was living the life I wanted to be living. I did not need someone to make me happy. The fashionista (or anyone else for that matter) could not fix my major challenges at the time: problems at work, a low back so painful that I could not stand for more than thirty minutes, and a fraught relationship with my mom, whose mental and physical health was worsening by the day.

Unbeknownst to me, I was transforming from single to Solo.

Fundamentally, that is what this book is about: a reinvention. I present a blueprint to create an identity that transcends relationship status by which to launch a remarkable life. While my transformation has taken me decades of work, I strive to speed along your reinvention.

Whether a lone wolf or the life of the party, Solos see themselves as complete—as a whole person. The typical single, the one with that false-but-familiar narrative running through his or her mind—marriage good, single bad—is waiting and hoping for a "better half" to come along, complete them, and make life better. Solos, however, neither see single living as liminal nor lower status. They revel in their singularity.

Solos embrace autonomy, sovereignty, and self-reliance, while forging a connection with a broader community. They seek to provide for their own needs and view relationships—romantic or platonic—as a means to enhance life rather than repair it. Not all singles are Solos, and not all Solos are single. The Solo mindset is independent of relationship status. Solos can move in and out of romantic relationships without losing their identity.

Finally, Solos question the assumptions that govern romantic relationships. They recognize that not everyone wants or needs to partner up and settle down. Solos also question "the rules" more generally. They are comfortable with values and lifestyles that diverge from convention. In the same way that they do not default into a romantic relationship, Solos revel in being politely unconventional.

To go Solo is to recognize that being single is the natural state in the world. The individual is to be appreciated. To go Solo is to stop waiting and start living the life you want now. (Cue Mae West again.)

The transformation from single to Solo won't be easy. But when successful, the transformation has a cascading effect beyond sex, dating, and romance. As age forty approached, and suspecting my future would not include a family, I could have bought a Trans Am and started growing weed. Instead, I took the time, money, and energy that would have been dedicated to a family and used it to pursue a remarkable life—my remarkable life.

The word "remarkable" is an adjective used to describe something or someone that is noteworthy, extraordinary, or exceptional. A remarkable life is worthy of comment. If you choose a life that is remarkable to you, don't expect the remarks to always be positive. What does it mean to live remarkably? At its core, a remarkable life is chosen—aligned with personal goals, tastes, values, and lifestyle. There is no one remarkable life. There are remarkable lives. Behavioral scientists call this heterogeneity, or as my mom used to say, "Different strokes for different folks."

A remarkable life is not just about how people spend their time; it is about how people feel about how they spend their time. A person could be leading what appears externally to be an ideal life, but they may be battling discontent. Conversely, a person leading a seemingly ordinary life may be brimming with joy.

The same way one's feeling about being single is more important than being single itself, process matters more than outcome. What makes a life remarkable isn't determined by the finish line, but by the progression toward full potential. The closer your progress aligns with your potential, the more remarkable your life becomes.

My journey to develop my Solo status has progressed alongside my career as an academic. As a behavioral scientist and business school professor, I began my career researching the interplay of judgment, emotion, and choice, specifically researching moral psychology and what makes things "wrong." But as an assistant professor, I stumbled across an opportunity to answer a 2,500-year-old question, "What makes things funny?" With my tenure prospects already in doubt, I went all in on the humor research, founded the Humor Research Lab (aka HuRL), crisscrossed the globe to figure out what makes things funny, wrote books, hosted podcasts, created a game show, and performed at a professional comedy club. A colleague called my choice to crack the humor code a "career killer."

Along the way, I managed to repair my relationship with my mom, heal my aching back, and earn tenure. Nevertheless, I battled an internal narrative that I was bad at relationships. "Commitment-phobe." "Selfish." "Peter Pan."

As I drew my humor code project to a close, I found myself drawn to my most meaningful work: helping singles live remarkably. I launched *Solo*, a podcast that celebrates the opportunities of being single. Given that few podcasts were talking about singlehood in positive terms, I was unsure about the response. Soon enough, singles started sliding into my DMs—not to date me, but to thank me. A message from a listener said, "After discovering your podcast, my eyes have been opened to the reality that I don't need someone to be whole, that I can lead a great life, not in spite of but because of being single." Another listener concluded a note of thanks with a heartfelt sentiment: "I'm so glad you were born." Cue more crying.

Since then, the Solo project has exploded. I've hosted Solo Salons, mixers inspired by the French salons of the eighteenth century. Proud singles come together to socialize and experience talks, comedy, poetry, music, and dance. I have a research project called *Single Insights* that examines how singles are overlooked and undervalued in the marketplace. I even appeared on the *Today Show* with Maria Shriver to talk about the Solo movement. Another colleague chastised me for spending too much time on the Solo project. But I wouldn't stop. Couldn't stop. I am obsessed.

I started the project with three questions. First, I was curious why the experiences of remarkable singles contrasted so starkly with the conventional wisdom and perspective of popular culture. Why did our lived realities differ so drastically from society's perceptions? Second, I was fascinated by society's narrow focus on one type of acceptable romantic relationship, often culminating in marriage. If someone wants to break the rules and have an unconventional relationship or no relationship at all, how might they overcome the myths, stigma, and discrimination? The third question was for those who forgo the conventional route of partnering up and settling down. What other roads lead to a remarkable life? What fulfilling lifestyles exist beyond this one style of romance—and the American Dream more generally?

People who pursue marriage (or its long-term equivalent) benefit from society's approval, government policies, religious support, relationship counselors, and a zillion self-help books. Everyone is eager to help. Everyone except divorce lawyers. The same level of support does not exist for singles. Too many books for singles are about how to "couple up" or "cope." If you want one that does both, pick up a copy of *How to Date Men When You Hate Men.*

This book is for *all* singles—whether you are single by choice or single by chance, whether you have never married, are separated, divorced, or widowed. Maybe you are tired of feeling out of place. Maybe you are excited about a new approach to living because the rules do not work for you. Maybe you've noticed a recurring pattern of unsuccessful relationships and are seeking insights or even an alternative to the traditional relationship path. Maybe you just want to better understand your world.

In a relationship, but still reading? Fret not, the Solo movement has a big tent. Not all Solos are single. Perhaps you've realized that you may not be partnered for long. Perhaps you are dating but wish to have more independence. Perhaps you want more alone time. Perhaps you are mismatched with your partner and want to find a way to change the rules.

Allies are welcome. Are you a parent or an educator trying to impart wisdom and guidance to young people who are starting their journey toward adulthood? A member of a community or religious group aiming to understand and support single members? A mental health professional or a life coach seeking to expand your tool kit to assist single clients? Need a book to give a friend who texts you the same dating dilemmas over and over?

Whatever way you got here, welcome! There is much to share and learn on the road from single to Solo to remarkable living.

As I began my research, I was surprised by how enormous and complicated the topic of single living is. To understand the implications of singlehood for the individual and society requires an understanding of psychology, sociology, anthropology, demography, economics, political science, and history. I'll present findings that reveal the unsung benefits of solitude, demystify the paradox of marriage—a revered institution that often serves society more than the individual—and present the opportunities and challenges single people face in a world built for two.

My experimental training taught me to question conventional wisdom and correct the record when marriage advocates mislead with statistics. I have conducted my own research, surveying singles and non-singles alike. I will share those results, as well as the many reasons behind the striking rise in single living, including how happy singles beget more happy singles.

**My thesis: Singlehood is not as bad—and marriage is not as good—as you've been led to believe.** Whether you find my assertion unpleasant or self-evident, the science backs me up.

I am not anti-marriage. I just think this *one type* of relationship is overprescribed. Matrimony is ideal for some people and disastrous for others. I know people who are built for marriage; they have wonderful relationships and would despair without a partner. I know people who have had bad luck in their relationship and wish to be free of it. I know sad, lonely, single people waiting and hoping to find "the one." I know people who are living their best lives unapologetically unattached. I also know marriage is just one of many ways to live a remarkable life.

Relationships and morality go hand in hand. Consequently, we are going to quickly bump up against behaviors that you or others instinctually find to be "wrong." My standard for whether something is wrong depends on two conditions: consent and harm. If there is consent between parties and no harm is being caused, then people should be free to do what they want. The former is easy to judge. The latter is more difficult. If it were easy, we wouldn't have philosophers.

So, to help navigate the ideas herein, I ask for three things:

**Vulnerability.** There are rewards and risks when one strays from the conventional path of securing a degree, landing a job, marrying, buying a house, starting a family, and hoping to make it to retirement. The insights presented here are primarily descriptive, meant to outline possibilities rather than dictate a prescription. Thus, the real success lies in identifying what makes your life remarkable and being comfortable with it, even when it doesn't align with societal norms. Be brave.

**An abundant mindset.** It is difficult to change your mind, but it is often easier to change your mind than your situation. Your challenges and opportunities are determined, in part, by birthplace, gender, race, religion, sexual orientation, class, and ability. A remarkable Solo life for a woman in Saudi Arabia is different than for a woman in Sweden. Your path may be harder or easier than others. Nevertheless, research reveals that people who focus on opportunity rather than limitations are more likely to succeed. They are happier, too.

**An open mind and heart.** I present a wide array of perspectives including those of asexuals, polyamorists, and relationship anarchists. Many ideas will be contrary to what you've learned to be appropriate. In the same way that people may not approve of your unconventional choices, their choices may challenge your values and beliefs. Please explore differing beliefs and behaviors with curiosity and compassion. This won't be easy, and that's okay.

Am I the ideal guide for this rather personal, even controversial, journey? Nope. I have had sloppy one-night stands and bad breakups that I regret. My personality and opinions are not for everyone. My friend Julie tells her friends who are about to meet me, "My friend Peter is going to be there. He's not for everyone." Despite my own personal growth and professional perspective, I still have the limited experience of being a straight, white, middle-aged American male who went to college, grad school, and works in the insular world of academia.

Fortunately, I have an amazing, diverse group of friends, experts, lovers, colleagues, and Solo community members who contribute to my perspective. They challenged me to grow. You will meet some of them—some in the form of Solo Love Letters throughout the book. I thank them for their generosity.

Despite my flaws and rough edges, I am here to guide you along your journey—from single to remarkable Solo.

Let's get started!

# ONE

# Human Domestication

The Game of Life was invented by Milton Bradley in 1860. An educator and religious man, Bradley created the iconic spinner because he associated dice with gambling. The original version was called The Checkered Game of Life due to the game's checkerboard setup and life's checkered path of rewards and risks such as wealth, poverty, happiness, or misfortune. There was even a space for "Duel," which evidently still occurred in 1860.

The Game of Life underwent a dramatic revamp in 1960 for its hundredth anniversary. Though the spinner remained, the updated version looks little like the original, which was focused on the pursuit of virtue. The revamp reflected 1960s optimism. Players "spin to win" and move their game pieces—brightly colored automobiles—around the game board, encountering life events along the road: get a job, get married, have children, and retire at Millionaire Acres. You know, pursue the American Dream.

The Game of Life features a shocking lack of freedom. Reflecting the conformity of the day, only a few places on the board offer a fork where players choose the road they want. For example, players can choose the "Family path," which results in one or more children, or a childless "Life path." Whereas the original version left matrimony to chance, the 1960 version made matrimony mandatory. Players make a perfunctory stop at a designated spot and add either a pink or blue spouse peg to the passenger seat of their car. I recall there was something strangely satisfying about that act, as though I had accomplished something special.

Mandatory marriage was not a far-out concept in 1960, when 90% of American adults were either married or would eventually marry. (The average age of first marriage was just twenty-one.) Few accomplishments come close to those proportions. The turnout for the Kennedy/Nixon election was 62 percent, church attendance was 63 percent, and the high school graduation rate was 65 percent. Since then, graduation rates have gone up, church attendance has gone down, and voter turnout remains roughly the same.

Marriage rates have since gone down—way down. Yet, society today still feels like 1960 in a lot of ways—built for two. To understand how the world came to be built for two—and a particular type of two—we need to go back a few million years to meet Lucy and learn what makes humans unique in the animal kingdom.

Unearthed by paleoanthropologists in the Afar region of Ethiopia in 1974, Lucy is a remarkably well-preserved fossil of a female *Australopithecus afarensis* hominin, which roamed the earth on two legs between 3.9 and 2.9 million years ago. Lucy's discovery was an important moment in understanding what makes humans unique. Like her human descendants—who have been around for 2.9 million years, and early *Homo sapiens* (us), who have been around for 200,000 million years—she lived the hunter-gatherer life.

Lucy might have pair bonded, the creation of strong emotional attachments between individuals, and she may have had children. However, if she wanted a walk down the aisle, she would have to wait about three million years till 2350 BCE, when the first documented marriage between a man and a woman occurred in Mesopotamia. For those of you who don't want to look at a map, Mesopotamia is where Iraq, Kuwait, Turkey, and Syria are now located. For those of you who don't want to do the math, that was just 4,377 years ago.

To put this all into perspective, matrimony—which is so pervasive and such an important milestone in a human's development—has only been around for a small part of history. Prior to its invention, single was the natural state of the world.

Well before inventing "domestic bliss," humans managed to establish themselves as the undisputed apex predators on a global scale. How did they achieve this extraordinary dominance? Not by brute strength or exceptional speed or the ability to throw a spear; rather from an exceptional ability to cooperate and create culture.

Humans are highly cooperative, a fact that might seem surprising if you spend any time on social media. The roots of this cooperation were most apparent in hunting and foraging behaviors. Humans established a division of labor based on individual skills, effectively creating a prehistoric assembly line. This structure greatly enhanced cooperation and improved food sources. Better nutrition led to bigger brains. Bigger brains led to better learning, teaching, and planning. All of this created a flywheel of optimization and innovation, which was critical to the development of culture.

The development of "mentalizing," being able to understand that others may possess different knowledge, was an essential element of cooperation and the creation of culture. Mentalizing is fundamental in the transmission of valuable information, enabling one person to discover something and then pass that knowledge on to others. Other animals can't do that—and not just because they don't have Wikipedia. Language further aided the rise of cultural learning, but it can only get so much credit. Whereas language appeared in our species fifty thousand years ago, mentalizing has been around for nearly two million years.

The ability of humans to invent and adopt not just physical inventions, such as fire, the wheel, and air fryers, but cultural practices set our species far apart from other animals. We are cultural learners. In his book *The Secret of Our Success,* Joseph Henrich emphasizes that the capacity of humans to learn and teach is foundational to our societal achievements and struggles. According to Henrich, culture is "the large body of practices, techniques, heuristics, tools, motivation, values, and beliefs that we all acquire while growing up, mostly learned from other people."

From the invention of fashion to Formula One and basketball to breakdancing, culture makes our world interesting and entertaining, expanding what makes life worth living beyond a tasty meal or the pleasures of the flesh.

From the first "artist" drawings on a cave wall to a stand-up comedian filling a club with laughs, culture allowed humans to develop other ways to stand out besides hunting or foraging well—which is good. Can you imagine your coworkers attempting to spear a wooly mammoth rather than stealing your lunch from the office fridge?

Cultural learning manifested in tangible forms, like techniques to trap a mastodon in a swamp for an easier kill (silly mastodon!). Conversely, other cultural elements are intangible "fictions"—imaginative stories and shared beliefs, highlighted by Yuval Harari in his book *Sapiens: A Brief History of Humankind.* As societies became more complex and less connected, strangers began interacting at a grand scale and needed fictions—myths, religion, and folklore—to make sense of the world and enhance cooperation.

Money, democracy, the stock market, college degrees, land ownership, and even the concept of being "cool" are all examples of fictions that hold significant societal importance. These fictions are often referred to by scholars as "social constructs." I prefer Harari's term because "fictions" serve as a stark reminder that many things that seem so important are simply *made up.*

I use the zombie apocalypse test to tell the difference between tangible facts and made-up fictions: During an apocalypse, culture crumbles. Bullets still hurt and orgasms remain delightful, but the fictions that connote success and status—a degree from Harvard or homeownership—are rendered meaningless. What matters is the immediate reality. "Can you build a fire?", "Can you suture a wound?", and the very important, "Are you good at killing zombies?"

Setting aside the zombie apocalypse and looking back at how humanity evolved, one cannot ignore our extraordinary ability to create order from chaos through cultural learning.

Humans are domesticators and the domesticated.

We are rule-making machines. Consider how we domesticated wolves into lapdogs in less than fifteen thousand years, rewarding good behavior and punishing bad to establish harmony. We, too, are also rule-obeying machines. We create laws, norms, and customs that facilitate effective cooperation and help societies to function.

Some rules are explicitly defined and written down, such as laws. Others are unwritten yet widely recognized social norms. Unwritten rules are more numerous and largely enforced through social means. Children as young as three effortlessly learn and abide by these norms based on observation, requiring no explicit teaching. Children even enforce them, expressing disapproval when the rules are broken. Adults, too, are quick to pass judgment when someone breaches these norms—look at social media for ample examples.

The problem with "the rules" lies in their variable nature. Many are arbitrary, some are harmful, and others are grounded in flawed convention. However, convention constantly evolves because of scientific evidence and cultural progress. Surgeons now wash their hands before surgery, unmarried women are no longer considered witches, and for better or worse, cocaine is no longer available in Coca-Cola.

Now, let's pretend to play The Prehistoric Game of Life. You got the latest loincloth, whittled your tools, and your tribe is developing a more complex culture. You've spun the spinner and had the good fortune of taking a great leap forward. You get to farm! This path only became possible after the smart people of Mesopotamia's Fertile Crescent started cultivating wheat, barley, and lentils in 12,000 BCE. Again, if you don't want to do the math, that was 14,024 years go.

Settling down to farm and rear livestock was a logical choice. Agriculture enabled the storage of food for scarce times, offering a more stable and reliable food supply. While farming solved a set of problems, it also introduced profound challenges related to cooperation, land ownership, reproduction, child-rearing, and division of labor. In response, societies developed new rules and inventions.

Among these inventions was the institution of marriage.

Now that you have a farm, it's time to spin to win and find a mate. Yet the rules of The Prehistoric Game of Life dictate that you don't get to select which peg lands in your carriage. Your spouse is chosen for you by your family, perhaps with input from the community. Indeed, the first marriages were arrangements— a practical invention that structured family life, regulated parenthood, and constructed strategic alliances. In large part, arranged marriages were conceived to establish "in-laws."

The irony that anyone would *want* in-laws is not lost on me.

Arranged marriages, much like business agreements, were legal partnerships centered on consolidating land, wealth, and power. They united families who shared a vested interest in the prosperity of their farms, businesses, and offspring. This alliance effectively replaced a tribal structure with extended family structures focused on the business of farming.

The agrarian age gave rise to patriarchy—a system in which men hold vast power and predominance in society. Marriage was invented by men, and women were treated as property, with their lives, earnings, and even their sexuality controlled by husbands. Dowries and economic transfers commodified women. In some extreme examples, women were kidnapped and turned into brides.

How did the patriarchy occur? The answer lies in the change to gender-based division of labor. The division of labor, which is one of humanity's defining characteristics, became more oppressive with farming. Gender-based cooperation was prevalent in hunter-gatherer societies. Women tended to forage, gathering fruits and nuts, while men hunted (notably, there was some overlap in roles). Because both hunting and foraging were critical to survival, tribes were relatively more egalitarian. However, a gender-based division of labor was not equally valued within farming. Men assumed roles that required physical strength, such as plowing, harvesting, and animal husbandry, while women engaged in domestic chores and child-rearing, which were less valued.[1]

The first arrangements between brides and grooms were rooted in practicality, not love. The wife in an arranged marriage hoped her husband would be kind and not abuse her. At best, she hoped that a loving relationship might arise. Nevertheless, these marriages typically resulted in large families. While it's often suggested that the high birth rate was intended to provide extra hands for farming, the parsimonious explanation is a lack of reliable birth control. More important, children ensured that wealth stayed within the family lineage.

Men experienced increased mobility in the agrarian age, often needing to travel for trade or to pursue new opportunities. Women were primarily responsible for domestic tasks and child-rearing. Marriage created cultural and legal guardrails designed to ensure that men would return home and remain involved in their children's lives, thus preserving family lineage. In essence, fathers were more likely to stay put if there were consequences for leaving, such as child support obligations, and if they had assurance that their children were indeed theirs, as enforced by rules of monogamy. No need for Maury Povich to reveal that indeed you were the father.

Historians widely believe that monogamy became dominant for Western marriages sometime between 500 and 800 CE. The rise of monogamy was pushed foremost by the Christian church in conjunction with arranged marriages. Monogamy thus facilitated clear inheritance lines (i.e., "These are my kids"). Moreover, the need to be consistent (i.e., 'til death) was often vowed publicly before family, friends, and God, which helped keep men invested in the family.

In hunter-gatherer tribes, partnerships often formed based on mutual attraction, leading to pair bonding; however, such bonds rarely lasted a lifetime. (Anybody who has moonwalked out of a relationship as quickly as they danced in already knows this.) Research suggests that the typical length of pair bonding is one to three years, hence the term "honeymoon phase." Once the honeymoon phase ended in hunter-gatherer times, it wasn't as simple as a father deciding to "step out for a pack of cigarettes" and never return. First, there were no convenience stores, and second, to go it alone was a death sentence.

I will spare you the description of The Industrial Age Game of Life. However, it's worth noting that the Age of Enlightenment in the seventeenth and eighteenth centuries in Europe brought significant changes to how "players" married.

The pragmatic arrangement of marriages began to give way to the novel concept of love marriages. People began to see marriage as a means for personal fulfillment, rather than merely a strategy for social and financial security.[2]

The Enlightenment, boasting prominent figures such as John Locke, Voltaire, Immanuel Kant, Olympe de Gouges, Ben Franklin, and Mary Wollstonecraft, was a philosophical and intellectual movement that valued reason, empiricism, and individualism, set against the backdrop of burgeoning independence and financial security caused by industrialization and urbanization. People began leaving their family farms to work in cities, which was particularly empowering for women (the original *Sex and the City*). Women worked in a range of professions—clerical work, service jobs, servitude, even sex work—some of which allowed them to out-earn men. As women gained greater financial independence and rights, the idea of marrying for love rather than family interests became more acceptable, even desirable.

As love-based marriages became more common, in the mid-nineteenth century, people started choosing partners based on shared interests and values, a shift away from mere social status or economic considerations. The advent of love marriages led to new inventions and practices, such as dating rituals. It eventually led to new societal structures, most notably the nuclear family, which became especially prominent during the post–World War II era.[3]

The popular media of the 1950s, including shows such as *Leave It to Beaver* and *Father Knows Best,* portrayed this nuclear family structure as the ideal: a homemaker mother, a breadwinner father, a house, and a car in the suburbs. I also recall there was a lot of pipe smoking.

The nuclear family structure was facilitated by a cascade of societal changes. Industrialization moved people from rural, extended family structures, placing them in cities where smaller families were more practical. Moreover, work moved outside the home and into a breadwinner model, which enforced a gendered division of labor within families that furthered the patriarchy. Mobility increased due to job demands, and smaller families were also better adapted to swiftly shifting circumstances. However, the nuclear family model is often misunderstood and overrated. Many families in the post–World War II era failed to reach the American Dream that they watched on their black-and-white TVs. In fact, today's percentages of homeownership, car ownership, and college degrees are higher than they were in the 1950s.

Reducing the family unit to a small and insular structure had its drawbacks. It is isolating and risky. Robert Putnam's book *Bowling Alone* discusses how the decline of community participation during this era led to increased loneliness. The homemaker role for women was not only isolating, but also continued the subservience of wives to husbands. Moreover, compared to arranged marriages, the nuclear family was at greater risk of fracturing due to death or divorce. Divorce rates also increased. Indeed, when love within a love marriage fades, so does the major motivation to stay together. Children often bear the brunt of the repercussions. I was one of those children.

In the 1960s and beyond, marriages began to further evolve into "growth" marriages, a concept that gained popularity and promoted self-discovery and personal growth. This era, characterized by the rise of psychotherapy, increased use of psychedelics, and a blossoming self-help movement, marked a cultural shift toward valuing self-expression, self-discovery, and self-actualization. People started to look for a life partner who would align with their goals and aid their personal and professional growth. Expectations for what constituted an acceptable lifelong partner went way up.

Eli Finkel, the author of *The All-or-Nothing Marriage: How the Best Marriages Work*, presents a metaphor for the growth marriage: This partner is to be your "everything," from yoga partner to forming a power couple. Imagine a freight train where emotional fulfillment is the single engine pulling multiple cars, each representing companionship, financial stability, shared goals, and similar lifestyles. Emotional fulfillment is the driving force. That is a lot for an engine to pull and, well, you know what happens if the engine breaks down. (I suspect his choice not to title his book *The Freighted Marriage* was a good one.)

While the shift from arranged marriages to love marriages has generally been beneficial, especially for women, the all-or-nothing model of the growth marriage started collapsing under the weight of cultural expectations almost as soon as it was invented. Marital satisfaction in the United States has been declining since 1965. The desire to find someone who can provide everything—emotional, intellectual, social, and sexual fulfillment—is enticing, but challenging to achieve. When I consider my flaws, I have a tough time imagining how I could be the perfect person for anyone (remember my friend Julie's warning about me). Finkel presented me his perspective on how high the bar is with a cheeky anecdote: "Dave's a good man and he's a good father, but I don't feel like I'm growing as a person, and I'm not going to *suffer* that for the next thirty years."

In my lifetime, I have observed the breathtaking evolution of technology, from the clatter of electric typewriters to the silent chat responses of artificial intelligence. These advancements stir my imagination and stand in contrast with institutions that are slow to change and yet exert substantial influence over people's lives: educational institutions, the judicial system, and the institution of marriage.

Marriage is a small part of human existence, but it has a profound effect on society today. Nevertheless, I have also witnessed a shift in marital norms. Not long ago, my friends at the lunch table believed marriage was about when and not if. The conversations on the text message threads of today are more about "if."

Whether marriage should be on the rise or the decline depends on your belief about the goodness of marriage as a tool for society and a means to a remarkable life. Historically, marriage was (and in some places still is) a business arrangement, thus casting this institution in a different light. This understanding of the evolution and iterations of marriage should empower people to question whether society's prescriptions align with their aspirations and values. As our understanding of life expands, it follows that our perception of life's rules should also change.

The Game of Life is a cultural artifact that reflects societal norms and trends of its time. It subtly domesticated me into blind acceptance of a particular set of life rules, including getting married and pursuing the proverbial American Dream. Society often goes a step further, framing marriage as the righteous choice—the ideal path to success, happiness, and fulfillment. I am eager to see future versions of the game that allow for more diverse life choices, much like the recent revision that presents players the choice to marry or remain single.

Going Solo is a courageous act that defies domestication. Solos audaciously craft a life uniquely their own. They ask whether institutions serve the individual or society. They question the rules, striving to understand how these norms are invented and influential. Equipped with this knowledge, Solos can begin to free themselves by either bending the rules or breaking them, when necessary.

## SOLO LOVE LETTER

### Mary, Writer, Los Angeles, California, USA

First grade. We were scribbling away on tables strewn with construction paper and mangled crayons. The teacher had told us to draw ourselves as adults. Lost in my drawing, I finally looked up and realized I had done something wrong. Everyone else had drawn multiple people. Their misshapen stick figures each had a partner and two or three malformed children. I was the only one at my table who had drawn one (disfigured) person holding a book, because I believed my future self would be an author.

I wasn't trying to be rebellious. It simply hadn't occurred to me to draw a family and kids, and I was surprised that everyone else had drawn versions of the same thing. I'm still not sure whether my classmates were influenced by the acculturation of family values, or whether they were genuinely excited to become parents. Maybe both.

I just know that I never wanted to have kids, and never will.

Aside from a short-lived fear of failing first-grade drawing, I've never felt "wrong" or deficient for not wanting to give birth. When people ask me why I don't want kids, I ask them politely why they do.

It's interesting how many people seem taken aback or even uncomfortable at having to answer the same question they just asked me. I bet for many it's the first time they have been asked.

People walking the path well-traveled rarely need to defend themselves, but often feel comfortable asking others to explain their life choices. I don't mind having to explain. Single by choice at thirty, I'm proud (and I have fun stories).

## SOLO LOVE LETTER

### Craig, Professor and Author of
### *How to be a Happy Bachelor,* Washington, DC, USA

"I just want to be friends." Three times in a year I had been told that by a dating partner, and each time those words crushed me. My funk would last a couple of weeks.

Thirty-seven and single, I was down because society was telling me to feel that way. There was clearly something wrong with me for being single. One humid summer afternoon, with this narrative stuck in my brain, I typed "being single as an adult" into Google. That search lead me to Dr. Bella DePaulo.

DePaulo had written articles and books about the stigma surrounding single people, and coined two terms: 1) *singleism*, the discrimination and marginalization faced by singles; and 2) *matrimania*, the societal obsession around marriage and coupling. I spent the next few hours down the rabbit hole of information related to how singles are perceived in our society, and then the light bulb went off in my head: I felt crappy about being single, because that was the message I had internalized my entire life.

Being single has freed me to experience things I never would have had I coupled. I've had the privilege of moving around the United States for my career, traveled to Malaysia and beyond, built many meaningful relationships, developed hobbies, and even dated interesting people in a much healthier way than I did before I discovered the joy of being Solo.

Our world places way too much emphasis on coupling; movies, song lyrics, books, political rhetoric, even academic research falsely tells us that we need to pursue romance. As I live my best Solo life, I also aim to show others that single living can be done well. Through writing about the way I live, I aim to help singles live well.

# TWO

# A World Built for Two

In the iconic *Sex and the City* episode "A Woman's Right to Shoes," Carrie Bradshaw, played by Sarah Jessica Parker, finds herself in a quandary. She is invited to a baby shower at her girlfriend Kyra's apartment, where guests are requested to remove their shoes before entering. Upon departing, Carrie is surprised to find that her luxury Manolo Blahnik shoes have been stolen. She asks her friend Kyra to reimburse her for the shoes. Stunned by the $485 price tag, Kyra offers her $200 and shames Carrie for spending that kind of money on shoes ("Chuck and I have responsibilities now").

The exchange prompts Carrie to reflect on the many times she's been expected to celebrate milestones in her married friends' lives, often involving costly expenditures on gifts and travel: "Over the years, I have bought Kyra an engagement gift, a wedding gift, then there was the trip to Maine for the wedding, and three baby gifts. In total, I have spent over $2,300 celebrating her choices. And she is shaming me for spending a lousy 485 bucks on myself?"

As an act of defiance, Carrie decides to marry herself. She puts one item on her registry: a replacement pair of Manolo Blahnik shoes.

Of course, marrying oneself won't bestow all the benefits of marriage. The world is built for two—and a particular type of two: a couple riding the **relationship escalator**.

To understand the escalator, I turned to my friend Amy Gahran, the author of *Stepping Off the Relationship Escalator: Uncommon Love and Life,* who happens to live not far away from me in Colorado. Her book offers a lens for people who are eager to understand relationships—and eager to break the rules to design relationships that better suit their individual needs.

According to Amy, the relationship escalator is the "default bundle of societal expectations that dictates a predetermined order of steps couples are expected to follow as they get more involved and committed to each other." I credit her for coining the term "relationship escalator," but she humbly admits that she heard it from someone else, although she can't recall who. Nevertheless, she gave the term structure and moved it into the public vernacular.

If you are on any dating apps you've surely seen the language people use when seeking to ride the relationship escalator:

Significant other.

Long-term relationship. LTR. Life partner.

A serious relationship. Something real.

My other half. My better half. My person.

Partner in crime. Ride or die.

The One.

An escalator ride occurs when two (and only two) people follow a progressive set of steps, often with distinct markers, toward a clear goal of "till death do us part." The escalator provides a script dictating the sequence of steps a couple is expected to follow as their commitment deepens.

Even without having taken the ride themselves, people know the exact steps and rules of such an escalator relationship, thanks to most romantic movies—*The Notebook, Love Actually,* and *The Big Sick* just to name a few. These movies follow a tradition predated by classic literature that depicted escalator-style relationships, even before escalators were invented, such as *Jane Eyre, The Great Gatsby,* and *Pride and Prejudice.*

Here is a refresher on the process (not that you need it):

- **Contact and initiation.** Flirting, casual dates, and maybe sex early on. Romantic courtship. Romantic gestures. "Catching feels." "Falling in love." "Swept off my feet."
- **Claiming and defining.** Mutual declarations of love. Coming out in public as a couple (i.e., becoming an item). Meeting each other's friends. Public displays of affection (PDA). Adopting possessive relationship labels (e.g., my boyfriend, my girlfriend). Ending other sexual and romantic relationships. Assuming or asking for sexual and romantic exclusivity. Forgoing barriers, such as condoms, if applicable.
- **Settling in and commitment.** Consciously or unconsciously crafting a social rhythm. Developing patterns for spending time together (e.g., date nights, sex, sleepovers). Creating norms for communication (a "good night" text may be required). Discussing or planning a future as a monogamous couple, as defined by the "Where is this going?" talk. Meeting each other's family.
- **Merging and conclusion.** Moving in together. Sharing finances. Getting engaged and married (common but not mandatory). The relationship is now complete and should remain intact until one partner dies. Terminating the relationship for any other reason is considered a failure by the couple and/or community.

- **Legacy.** Having kids and/or buying a home (in the United States, especially). Neither is as required as it once was, yet a couple may feel incomplete, or friends and family may see them that way, until these milestones are met.

The steps of the escalator may be proposed directly by a potential partner with requests such as "Let's be exclusive," "I want to move in," or "Will you marry me?" *Yes* or *maybe* are acceptable answers, but a *no* typically stops the escalator ride, as it has many times for me.

Children learn about the escalator through socialization processes at home and school. Family members and friends model and socially reinforce the steps. Schools contribute to this understanding through sex education and health classes, often implicitly teaching the steps while omitting the possibilities of any other romantic relationship. A 2017 study by the Guttmacher Institute found that 75 percent of US schools teach about monogamy; 44 percent teach about unconventional relationships, such as solo monogamy, polyamory, or sexual friendships.

The escalator is the standard by which most people gauge whether a romantic relationship is serious, committed, moral, and worth pursuing. There are steps and there are rules. The underlying rules of the escalator are likely familiar even if you do not personally subscribe to them.

## RULE 1: HIERARCHY

The escalator relationship should be the most important adult–adult relationship in the couple's life.

Hierarchy means status, and status means winners and losers. Coined by philosopher Elizabeth Brake in 2012, "amatonormativity" refers to the social and cultural assumption that a romantic relationship is the most important and valuable relationship in a person's life. Because an escalator relationship sits atop the hierarchy, it crowds out other relationships. Partners get prioritized for social events, vacations, attention, and affection. Partners often need to "check" to get an okay for social engagements outside of the escalator. The phrase "veto power" comes to mind.

In his research on interpersonal relationships, sociologist Harry Stack Sullivan coined the phrase "significant other." His original academic use included romantic partners as well as close friends, family, and mentors—anyone important in someone's life. Nowadays, the phrase is reserved for a single type of relationship: a committed escalator partner, whether married, engaged, or in a long-term relationship. By following that logic, everyone else is apparently "insignificant."

## RULE 2: MERGING

Escalator riders join their lives by way of living arrangement, finances, and even identity.

The idea of "two becoming one" is found in the Bible in Genesis 2:24—"the twain shall be one flesh," which emphasizes the bond between husband and wife. "One flesh" is more than just a physical union; it is about functioning as one unit.

A big, often exciting, step for escalator riders is to merge dwellings. Perhaps one person moves in with the other or they start fresh with a new place. Merging is made easier when people share similar tastes, temperature preferences, and standards of cleanliness. In fact, compatibility is often a major consideration in moving a relationship ahead (e.g., "Could I live with this person?" "I adore him, but he is such a slob. That will have to change.").

A couple will typically merge finances, perhaps taking turns paying for each other's expenses. They may open a joint bank account, a practice with historical roots dating back to early marriages in which a wife's possessions were owned by her husband.

Escalator riders start to incorporate their identity and lifestyles, which may be signaled through language: "We are adopting a pet." "This trip will be good for us." "Our diet is primarily plant-based these days." The riders may change their names. Although no longer required by law, about 70 percent of women in the United States give up their last name for their husband's. A merged identity may be signaled by some other name change, such as combining names. I call this the Bennifer phenomenon. Others invent their own names when they marry, sometimes making curious decisions, such as Meloharmony or McFlurry.

## RULE 3: CONSISTENT SEXUAL AND ROMANTIC MONOGAMY

The relationship is sexually and romantically exclusive with one and only one partner "till death do you part." The relationship is closed. Partners are not allowed to be intimate or romantic with others. Note: Monogamy does not guarantee intimacy or romance *within* the relationship. Ouch.

As Amy puts it, "To understand the relationship escalator is to understand the rules of the game. The expectations and timeline increasingly narrow the field of choice, funneling individuals to their inevitable end: merged and bound to another individual."

An escalator metaphor is an apt way to characterize this style of relationship. Just as it is easy to get on an escalator and awkward to get off, society encourages and rewards the riders (think of all those celebrations), while also thwarting the end to the ride (think of how freaking hard it is to get divorced). There are also behavioral phenomena that make it easy to get on and stay on the escalator. Here are three.

First up is the *progression bias,* a human tendency to favor actions that advance a goal. Research by psychologists Samantha Joel and Geoff MacDonald in the journal *Personality and Social Psychology Review* reveals this tendency in relationship contexts: Increasing investment in a romantic partner is easier and more exciting than ending a burgeoning relationship.

The progression bias leads to a paradox: People will settle for a suitable partner rather than start fresh to find a better match. Joel and MacDonald conducted a lab study in which participants were presented dating profiles, and their potential dates possessed at least one trait participants said they did not want in a partner (i.e., deal-breakers), yet 74 percent agreed to the date anyway. From an evolutionary point of view, our ancestors may have prioritized having any romantic partner over finding an ideal one for gene survival. Something is better than nothing.

My comedian friend Shane Mauss knows how hard it is to unwind a relationship. Shane falls in love fast and falls hard. He is quick to merge, moving in with a new girlfriend soon after the relationship starts. They build a fun life together, but around year three, things start to go sideways. When the relationship ends, he moves out, taking only his clothes despite having furnished the apartment.

He told me, "You think IKEA furniture is hard to put together? Try taking it apart."

Second, *sunk costs* contribute to people staying on the relationship escalator. People are sensitive about wasting investments of time, effort, and money in economic or social contexts.

The sunk cost fallacy comes into play when someone continues investing in a decision because of prior investment, despite the fact that current evidence suggests it's not worthwhile to continue the investment. The greater the previous contributions, the stronger the commitment to the course.

Often, the sunk cost fallacy occurs because people incorrectly prioritize unrecoverable costs when, realistically, only future costs versus benefits should matter. Samantha Joel puts this in perspective: "Often, by the time you've figured out that your partner has some traits or life goals that are incompatible with yours, you've already invested substantially in that relationship. At that point, it's much harder to cut your losses. We don't like to waste our time and energy, and relationships take a lot of both."

This behavior is not dissimilar to the business concept of "throwing good money after bad," a phrase used to describe the act of continuing to invest money in a failing project because of the sunk costs. In relationships, this might manifest as "throwing good time after bad," persisting in a relationship that no longer serves us well.

The third reason the escalator is easier to get on than off is the *status quo bias*, or default bias. People are comfortable with what everyone else is doing and find it difficult to go against the grain. When people consider an option outside the default, they often focus on the downsides more than the upsides. Ending a relationship looms larger than the opportunity of a fresh start; this tendency goes by the name *loss aversion*, or *negativity bias*.

As the world nudges folks down the aisle, most people don't think to question whether they will do it—just *how* and *when* they will do it (like the guys at my lunch table did). One of those people was my dad. When I asked him why he got married, he shrugged his shoulders and said, "That's what you did."

## THE PRICE OF BEING SICK AND SINGLE

### A True Tale by Christina Campbell

"**Y**ou two are sitting on a gold mine," says my coworker Dave. He's trying to convince me and my close colleague Ada to get married, even though we are happily single, heterosexual women. Dave presents as a curmudgeonly ex-military dude, but sometimes his secret, kind streak surfaces. Today, he's trying to cheer me up by suggesting I commit insurance fraud.

He, Ada, and I are the sole occupants of the cubicle aisle next to the fridge. We're a little family, soothing and snarking at one another through the fabric panels between our desks. Of the hundred people in this office, Ada and I are part of a handful of single people. We work in government contracting, a culture not known for bucking social conventions, especially not the marriage-kids-two-car-garage trope.

"You guys need to get married," Dave says. "You check all the boxes." He points at Ada. "You're . . ." And at me: "And you're . . ."

"A woman of color," I say, gesturing to Ada, an Iraqi American. "And a disabled person." I point at myself, leaning on the snack counter because I'm aching and exhausted.

"And you'd be a gay couple," Dave says. "People would bend over backward for you." Ada looks amused and horrified.

Dave is correct—kind of. I doubt many people of color, disabled people, or LGBTQ+ couples think society bends over backward for them, but if those marginalized people paired up, they would at least be unconditionally encouraged to register at the local home goods store. Singles, on the other hand, aren't even encouraged to throw a graduate school shower, though it's arguably harder to find a thesis topic than a partner. I did consider having a sickness shower. I could have registered at Target for hot pads and bath salts—if I hadn't been afraid of being called selfish. Now Dave is saying it's Ada's and my turn to get free stuff. I'm listening.

More than a thousand US federal laws privilege married people over singles. A few years before my conversation with Dave, a friend and I wrote an article for *The Atlantic* describing how much a hypothetical single person would spend in a lifetime compared to his or her married peers, based on the marital status discrimination in these laws (such as Social Security and taxes). Answer: Easily at least $1 million. Now I'm seeing this play out in my own life, and Dave is trying to help.

The backstory: A coworker and I have similar chronic illnesses, so we work part-time. We therefore don't get employer-provided health insurance. She's married, and I'm single. She uses her husband's insurance. I have myriad friends who would let me mooch off their health plans—except we'd probably go to jail. Ergo, I pay $930 per month for COBRA coverage. In this tidy example of intersectional discrimination (ableism meets singleism), I pay over $11,000 more per year than my coworker, simply because she has a state-sanctioned-sex roommate, and I don't. The problem is, both relationship status and health are inherently random processes. You can't tie benefits to random processes. It's like trying to legislate the weather.

From my perch against the snack counter, I laugh at Dave's marriage scenario. He's encouraging me to buck the system, and that's refreshing. Most other people, when I complain about marital status discrimination, tell me to fall in line. "So, just get married, then," they say, in all seriousness. They seem to think I can just stroll around and find a well-insured person with whom to tie the knot. Which is ridiculous.

Or is it?

## BENEFITS OF GETTING HITCHED

In most places in the world, an escalator ride takes on special significance when it is marked by marriage. I am going to use financial benefits of marriage in the United States as a case study of incentives, but the things incentivizing people to ride are much more pervasive.

Let's start with a counterintuitive anecdote that reveals how motivating financial benefits can be.

Liana Wolk, a teacher, and Owen Marshall, a musician, found themselves in front of a Portland, Maine, judge attempting a divorce for the second time in a month. The first judge rejected their request.

As it turned out, the couple's decision was not driven by infidelity or marital discord, but by a loophole in the Affordable Care Act. Dubbed the "family glitch," a provision penalized five million married Americans by requiring them to pay higher premiums for health insurance coverage compared to their single counterparts.

The happily married Wolk and Marshall were wrecking their finances paying an insurance premium of $16,000 per year. Owen said, "We're just blowing through this money for no reason other than the stupid piece of paper that says we're married." As two single adults, however, they could each apply for individual coverage and lower their premiums. A second judge granted their request, and they divorced happily.

Wolk and Marshall's story is the exception that proves the rule, so to speak. If just one financial benefit of being single (or conversely, one financial cost of being married) could cause a happily married couple to divorce, imagine what more than a thousand legal benefits and protections provided by the government to married people might do to incentivize marriage. These benefits are vast: Receive your partner's Social Security benefits, have a company pay for your partner's healthcare, and possess the authority to make life or death decisions on your behalf. Benefits so vast that people have been known to enter into "marriages of convenience" or "contract marriages" to obtain immigration opportunities, healthcare, or tax benefits.

Christina Campbell is an advocate for singles and the cofounder of the blog *Onely* with Lisa Arnold. Fed up with the stigma that singles face, their aim is to support singles. Christina talked to me about the differential benefits that married people have over single people:

> *Lisa and I thought, "How much money are we losing because of these discriminatory laws and the tax code in Social Security and housing discrimination?" We did some informal math. We looked at a couple of hypothetical characters who earn a little bit of a high-average amount of income in Virginia. We looked at examples in the federal code of discriminatory laws and crunched the numbers to figure out how much these hypothetical people would be losing compared to their married counterparts. The higher of the two incomes, which is still a very moderate income for the state of Virginia, that hypothetical person lost at least $1 million.*

A gap of a million dollars is no trivial matter. The actual amount will depend on the individual and a bunch of assumptions that I am hesitant to make. Yet one thing is certain: Getting married commands sizable financial benefits—that is, after you pay for the wedding. Benefits that are often unearned, unfair, or unwarranted.

Some of the advantages that partnered people have over single people are mathematical. Partnered people halve some expenses—so-called fixed costs such as housing, automobiles, meals, and hotel rooms are shared by both parties. A friend's boyfriend jokes with her, "Everything we buy together is technically half off!"

Partnered people, moreover, have the potential for two incomes, and thus a hedge in the case of disability, unemployment, or some other financial shock. I recently came across a bio on a dating profile that said, "I think I'm finally ready to have dual income. It just makes the most sense."

So much for romance.

One of the primary legal and unquestioned financial benefits for married couples in the United States is the option to file their taxes jointly, which often results in a lower tax bill compared to filing separately, and the tax brackets for married couples filing jointly are wider than those for single filers. The result is that couples can take advantage of lower tax rates on a larger portion of their income, potentially saving them thousands of dollars.[1]

Bachelor taxes, which date back to ancient Greece and Rome, are evidence that the government uses the tax code to incentivize marriage. The government's primary aim when taxing bachelors was to dissuade men from leading single lives and incentivize them to marry and establish families. A fear of social disorder was another significant motivation; unmarried men were viewed as potential instigators of immoral, even criminal, activity. I spoke to John McCurdy, a history professor at Western Michigan University, who told me about an infamous bachelor tax in Maryland in 1756, which targeted wealthy bachelors over the age of twenty-five. These bachelors were considered "old" rather than "eligible" bachelors.

McCurdy told me: "There's something wrong with an old bachelor. You're probably wasting your money. The government is also taxing Madeira and billiards tables—they're taxing other things associated with the extravagant lifestyle of a bachelor who's very wealthy in society."

I am keeping my grouchiness to a minimum, but the annoying thing about tax breaks for married people is that they are often *less* needed since the couple can share expenses. A common, reasonable response is to note that married people are more likely to have children, and children are expensive. I get it, but shouldn't that be when tax breaks kick in? Moreover, there are already various benefits and credits that are designed to support families with children, such as the child tax credit and the earned income tax credit. Nevertheless, a recent article from the United Kingdom was comfortable asking, "Should we tax the childless?"

Social Security is another aspect of the financial benefits of marriage. The system, created in 1936 and amended in 1939, offers a spousal benefit in case of the death or disability of a career-spouse who has paid into the system. That is, an *added* benefit—single people cannot designate a beneficiary despite having paid the same amount into the system. And it's not just about death or disability. Non-career spouses who have *not* paid into the system can still collect up to 50 percent of their partner's benefit amount once they reach retirement age. For the sake of fairness, why shouldn't singles similarly be able to name a beneficiary, say, a sibling or friend?

Another element of the case is estate taxes. When a married person dies, their spouse can inherit their estate without incurring estate tax. The exemption amount is lower for singles, resulting in higher taxes on their inheritance. Furthermore, married couples can gift unlimited amounts of money to each other without incurring gift tax. Why can't I, as a bachelor, also designate someone to gift my money to without a tax?

Differences in financial benefits are similarly evident in corporate and organizational benefits, skewing in favor of married employees.

One day, I received a "WTF" email from a professor at another university. The subject line said "spousal default." She wrote: "Not to get too 'solo' on you, but this is ridiculous!"

She then quoted the language on her university's benefits portal: "Don't forget to review the Spousal Surcharge and change it to 'Waive' if not applicable. This $100-per-month cost is automatically set to 'Select.'" In other words, employees have to "opt out" rather than "opt in" to pay for a spouse during open enrollment. So, single employees who overlook that selection are charged $1,200 a year for a benefit they don't need and can't use.

Employees expect the same compensation and opportunities for the same quality and quantity of work, yet married people receive greater benefits (for being married). A 2021 survey by the Kaiser Family Foundation found that 97 percent of employers with two hundred or more employees offer health benefits to employees. Of those employers, 95 percent offer additional coverage for an employee's spouse. With additional dependents (including children up to age twenty-six), the differential benefit swells. The same KFF survey found the average annual premiums paid by the employer for health insurance were $6,346 for single coverage and $16,000 for family coverage. This difference is rarely passed on to single employees.[2]

In a striking example of differential benefits for the same work, married American soldiers receive a better Basic Allowance for Housing and superior housing options than single soldiers. The BAH increases with the number of dependents. Indeed, soldiers refer to married service members receiving better benefits and promotion opportunities as "married army." Some American soldiers even put up ads on Craigslist to find spouses who are interested in an arrangement.

Early HR policies and management practices were based on two assumptions. The first was that an employee would eventually marry and differences in how single employees are treated would even out. The second was based on the predominance of the nuclear family, with a lone breadwinner supporting a family at home. That was fine in 1960 when 90 percent of people married, but that is no longer the case.

As Carrie Bradshaw realized, the same premise is true for celebrations of couple-hood. There are the gifts for weddings, baby showers, and baptisms, not to mention the super annoying invention of gender-reveal parties. When everybody married this kind of arrangement was copacetic. Folks enjoy the give-and-take of mutuality (i.e., "You scratch my back, and I'll scratch yours when you tie the knot"), but those who remain resolutely single end up devoting a hefty chunk of their time and coin backing, bankrolling, and feting married folks.

A friend of mine calculated how much she spent to be a bridesmaid at one wedding. The engagement gift, night before wedding gift (it's a thing now for bridesmaids to get the bride a basket with candles, champagne, lingerie, etc.), wedding gift, bridesmaid's dress, shoes, flights to destination, and Airbnb totaled about $1,400. And that does not include the bachelorette party. I joke that there is nothing more selfish than a destination wedding. Then a friend told me about how her friend, who lives in New York City, wanted a bachelorette *weekend* in London. Good grief.

With more lifelong singles, the thousands of dollars spent on gifts, flights, and hotel rooms go unreciprocated, creating what Michal Kravel-Tovi and Kinneret Lahad identify in the journal *Sociology* as "exhausted gift givers."

I used financial benefits as an example of how the world is built for two, but that is just the start. Another example is religious access and inclusion. Most Americans are Christian, and marriage is often a sacrament highly celebrated on the path to heaven. In Mormonism, for example, marriage *is* the path to heaven. For some people, salvation is built for two.

As you know now, marriage is something society invented—a fiction—but its invention set off the need for countless other fictions, including laws, which end up having tangible benefits that two people who marry receive over two people who are single. Singles should understand and recognize how society is incentivizing them to couple up—at the very least so that they can honestly assess all their motivations for wanting to do it or not.

In sum, when you look at these benefits ("the ol' gravy train," as my friend's grandma would say) of tax breaks, incentives, gifts, and even access to heaven that reward coupling up, it's no wonder people tend to default to riding the escalator.

I didn't even want to write the second half of this chapter. Most singles will find what I say about benefits to be self-evident. They already feel the pain of paying. But before I begin building the case for why marriage is not the only option, I needed to show that the escalator is society's default option, and that is very much by design.

## SOLO LOVE LETTER

**Sarah, Management Consultant, Indianapolis, Indiana, USA**

**W**hen I was a kid, I didn't like Barbies or dolls. I never worked in a babysitting gig.

What I did instead was bury my head in novels and dream about the adult life I would write for myself. The family members who knew me well expected I would not have kids or stay in Indiana as an adult.

I didn't feel the challenges of being single until my late twenties, when my entire community began to follow the "path" and create families "of their own." I felt myself transitioning in the eyes of others from an intrepid twenty-something traveling the world and having sexy adventures to an immature woman with no "place" and failing to get in line. But I wasn't immature—post–quarter life crisis, I was becoming a respected personality within my company and becoming debt-free. I was navigating the minutiae of daily life and also foreign things in foreign places with the same sense of ease. I was building friendships and romantic relationships based on deep understanding, while also making major fitness gains.

And yet I felt an increasing burden of judgment from society. I felt it in words and actions directed at me, but mostly I felt it in the design of the world and its unexamined assumptions. I felt it in the assumptions of my still-single peers who knew that they would one day have a spouse and children and live within the confines of the relationship escalator lest they lose social support. After all, a nuclear family is today what a community once was.

My turning point came from something my therapist said in response to my discomfort with being a black sheep in society: "You have a deep sense of who you are, and most people don't have that. Please don't give that up."

Today, I count myself lucky to have had the personality that pushed me to discover who I was and remain faithful to it. I still recognize the cloak of belonging that following the traditional path affords a person, and I envy those who are able to truly enjoy it. I indulge in love with family, friends, and significant others, but I know I'm not meant to be a mother or faithfully ride the relationship escalator, and this excludes me from many social entry points. But I'm also aware of the growing voices of people who followed the "path" and are beginning to openly express their regret. The Solo movement has been revolutionary in helping us recognize our own growing ubiquity and rethink the ways one can design a life.

It takes strength for those of us who feel Solo on the inside to organize our lives Solo-ly on the outside in the face of an enormous and largely unspoken lack of support from a society designed for coupled people, but it is a path of deep peace and fulfillment that only comes from being true to oneself.

## SOLO LOVE LETTER

### Kerri, Librarian, Brisbane, Queensland, Australia

I am a fifty-year-old cishet woman who has been single for my entire life apart from a very brief relationship of nine months, which was six months too long. Finding the Solo community has been a game changer for me. It has given me the language to more accurately describe myself. Being a single, middle-aged woman in society is clearly an object of pity. But being a Solo woman, well, is awesome! Listening to the *Solo* podcast, I felt validated, and would find myself nodding fiercely and yelling "Yes!" It was reassuring to discover so many folks out in the wide world who felt similarly to how I felt.

Let me be clear: I have always felt happy and content at being single/alone/Solo, but society didn't want me to. It was hard to fight against that societal messaging and maintain my contentment and happiness; it was clearly outrageous that I dared feel like this.

I received the following messages about my lack of desire for marriage or children:

"You'll change your mind when you meet the right man."

"Children are amazing; you'll be a great mum."

"Aren't you scared of being alone?"

"You don't know what you're missing."

"You are being selfish."

Yet, I never wavered, because I knew what was right for me.

I have brightly colored tattoos and dye my hair a variety of candy colors, usually a variation of pink. I did this in my early forties, and it felt like I had finally transformed how I see myself internally to be reflected in my external self. I was told: "Oooh, you're brave. A lot of men won't like that."

My reply: "I do this to please myself."

# THREE

# Someday

An annual ritual. Aunt Sally is seated next to Thelma, the sole single at a holiday gathering. Three generations of family drink wine and catch up on the year as the patriarch carves a turkey. In an adjacent room, a boisterous table of kids eating chicken fingers and mac and cheese are occasionally shushed by the family's matriarch.

Thelma has crossed the country, fighting weather, traffic, and flight delays to be home for the holidays.[1] She is fitting in the meal between visits to see old friends, many with their own families now. Not that long ago, she was seated with the kids. Though graduated to the adult table, Thelma will still spend the night on the pull-out couch. Her married sibling gets the guest room for the length of the stay. She'll even wake up early to help with the kids because, well, they'll be in the living room anyway.

Among the chatter, Aunt Sally and Thelma begin their dance:

*Aunt Sally: "Thelma, it is so lovely to see you. I can't believe how long it has been. How are you, dear?"*

*Thelma: "Never better. I just got a promotion, closed on a cute condo, did the trek to Machu Picchu, and rescued a sweet dog named Levi."*

*Aunt Sally: "Oh. That is so nice, dear, but is there anyone special in your life?"*

## *SOMEDAY* SINGLES

Aunt Sally contentedly rides the relationship escalator—and hopes that Thelma will someday find someone special for the ride. For Sally and many others, marriage works. The world is built for them. They have the wind at their back—wind that won't be noticed unless they move in another direction due to divorce, death of a spouse, or choosing different goals as Thelma seems to have done.

*Somedays* are the hopeless romantics on the lookout for "the one" with whom they can build a future. The archetype of a *Someday* single permeates the media, with characters such as Bridget Jones from *Bridget Jones's Diary*, Ted Mosby from *How I Met Your Mother*, Charlotte York from *Sex and the City*, and Marianne Dashwood from *Sense and Sensibility*.

*Someday* singles are caught between exciting possibilities and inherent challenges of accomplishing their goal. Fortunately for them, goal-setting often leads to success. For instance, when people set a goal to lose weight, they tend to shed pounds. Goals focus one's efforts and foster accountability. Establishing S.M.A.R.T. objectives that are specific, measurable, achievable, relevant, and time-bound markedly enhances the likelihood of success.

However, goal setting is not a foolproof strategy. There are three potential drawbacks for singles who have the goal to ride the relationship escalator.

## Drawback 1. Less Than

One problem with goals is that having one creates an agreement with yourself to not be satisfied until the goal is achieved. You are in deficit until that fateful day.

Single living as a "less than" state of the world is reinforced by dinner conversations, stories, and even games played by children (e.g., "Old Maid").

"Significant other," "husband," and "wife" conjure up images of weddings, anniversaries, and lifelong monogamy. These words symbolize roles in time-honored tales of love and unity. They carry the weight of devotion, protection, and caregiving. Words that convey status.

In stark contrast, terms such as "single," "Peter Pan," or "old maid" tell a different story—a story that, more often than not, veers closer to tragedy than comedy. To examine the status difference between single and non-single living, I conducted a study with 203 Americans who judged twenty-six relationship-related labels. Respondents rated their feelings about each label (e.g., spouse, spinster, solo) on a scale from 0, "Extremely negative," to 100, "Extremely positive." Table 1 presents the results in descending order of positive feelings. The results are striking but not surprising.

There is much to unpack from these results. First, look at how good it is to be on the escalator. On the left-hand side of the table are labels associated with a partnership. They all received resoundingly positive ratings and are positioned in the upper third of the scale. Conversely, on the right-hand side, labels indicative of singlehood consistently ranked in the lower half of the scale.

There is considerably more variance in the labels related to singlehood. For instance, there is a forty-two-point difference between "Single" and "Incel" (involuntary celibate), whereas the

| LABEL | SCORE | LABEL | SCORE |
|---|---|---|---|
| Wife | 85 | Single | 51 |
| Husband | 84 | Solo | 50 |
| Life partner | 82 | Unmarried | 50 |
| Spouse | 82 | Bachelor | 50 |
| Significant other | 81 | Peter Pan | 41 |
| Married | 80 | Lone wolf | 39 |
| Bride | 80 | Widowed | 35 |
| Long term relationship | 79 | Separated | 30 |
| Girlfriend | 79 | Cat lady | 30 |
| Better half | 77 | Divorced | 25 |
| Groom | 76 | Spinster | 23 |
| Boyfriend | 73 | Old maid | 20 |
| My person | 70 | Incel | 8 |

**TABLE 1:** Perception of relationship status labels rated by 203 Americans on a scale of "Extremely negative" (0) to "Extremely positive" (100). Results highlight a clear preference for partners-related labels over those indicating singlehood, with labels denoting single women receiving more negative ratings.

range is only fifteen points from "Wife" to "My person." Another intriguing aspect was that the "Single," "Unmarried," and "Solo" received higher ratings compared to more descriptive labels like "widowed" or "divorced." This insight suggests that people can claim more empowerment by using the former to describe themselves. Guess which word I would suggest.

Moreover, an interesting pattern emerges in the right-hand column: Single women bear the brunt of the negativity. Not even the dreaded label "Incel" can tip the scales.

One of the striking aspects of the derogatory labels attributed to single women is how they are often dehumanizing, likening them to animals, particularly with connotations of cunning or sexuality. Terms like "fox" for an attractive woman or "vixen" for one deemed more lascivious. Older women who have sexual relationships with younger men are tagged as "cougars" or "snow leopards," drawing parallels to the predatory nature of these animals.

Terms like "birds," "chicks," and "hens" are used to describe women in a manner that diminishes them to their biological attributes. "Mares" and "fillies" are employed for tall or athletic women, whereas "kittens" and "bunnies" are reserved for those who are perceived as cute or petite. The most iconic bunny is the Playboy Bunny. For some, the bunny represented sexual freedom and empowerment. For others, it epitomized oppression and patriarchy.

For men, animalistic comparisons hint at a lack of domestication. In 1755, Benjamin Franklin asserted that "a man without a wife is but half a man," and is even reputed to have referred to single men as "incomplete animals." The irony is rich, considering Franklin himself was hardly an exemplar of marital fidelity. While married to Deborah Read, he was known to frequent French brothels and engaged in various relationships with women, including one of his wife's friends.

According to cultural stereotypes, men are like wild animals, untamed beasts that can barely be trusted to behave in polite company. In contemporary China, single men are sometimes referred to as "single dogs" (光棍狗 *guānggùn gǒu*), suggesting that single people, like dogs, are dependent on others for companionship.

Howard P. Chudacoff, author of *The Age of the Bachelor: Creating an American Subculture*, describes how in seventeenth-century

New England single men were called "rogue elephants," untethered and potentially dangerous. If you prefer a more workmanlike analogy, how about references to single men being "unyoked oxen"?

Men are beasts of burden, especially useful when put to work.

Even "Peter Pan," the pejorative used to describe bachelors like me, is animal adjacent. In Sir James Barrie's classic play, Peter Pan is a boy who never grows up, living in the magical land of Neverland. His name is a nod to the half-human, half-goat deity, Pan, from Greek mythology, who communicates with fairies and birds through his enchanted pipes. To me, however, Peter Pan has a solid plan: half-man, half-goat, part-time party animal.

In short, the message is clear—ride the escalator and move from the right column to the left. No longer be "less than."

## Drawback 2: Liminal

"Don't waste my time."

For singles with a goal to ride the escalator, "someday" can't come soon enough—as indicated by that prevalent phrase on the dating apps.

Liminality is the in-between moment where people are neither in their previous state nor a new one. Liminality in space serves as a bridge between places—like a lobby or an elevator. Liminality in time marks the span of transitional periods in a person's life, like the moment a clock strikes midnight on New Year's Eve. The time may be short, such as a graduation ceremony, or long, such as adolescence. Weddings are liminal moments and chapels are liminal places.

Waiting may involve savoring, anticipation, and excitement. It's great to have a vacation looming. However, waiting often implies a lack of power. Common queuing scenarios are wasted time: in line at the grocery store, a doctor's waiting room, or anxiously anticipating boarding a plane. People don't go to a hotel to ride the elevator.

The goal to ride the escalator, "waiting for the one," looms liminally over *Someday* singles (hence why I call them "Someday" singles). Waiting for a person to complete you—and missing out on all the other benefits of partnering up and settling down— can make the waiting game even more agonizing. In the context of feeling incomplete, liminality takes on a unique dimension. What might begin as a temporary state of anticipation can stretch into years, even a lifetime. It's like a never-ending elevator ride or an indefinite wait at the DMV.

For many *Someday* singles, life without a partner is liminal, with no guarantee that the wait will be temporary. Success is not uniform. Some people have the privilege of being more attractive, successful, wealthy, socially adept, emotionally and physically healthy, and live somewhere with other appealing singles. After all, a request to find a significant other requires someone else to say, "Yes."

Pew Research Center reveals that about half of single adults in the United States are not actively seeking sex or romance. For some singles, their stage in life is less amenable to pursuing a conventional relationship—take an eighteen-year-old college kid, a divorced empty nester (i.e., "been there and done that"), and the oldest person in the world, Maria Branyas, at the time of this writing, a 116-year-old Spaniard who has never smoked or drunk alcohol.

A minority but nontrivial number of singles not seeking to date cite difficulties:

- 18 percent: haven't had luck in the past
- 17 percent: feel like no one would be interested

- 17 percent: feel too old
- 11 percent: have health problems that make it difficult

According to the World Health Organization, more than one billion people around the globe—roughly 15 percent of the world's population—live with a disability of some kind. These disabilities may create additional barriers to forming relationships. For instance, people with physical disabilities may face hardships accessing public spaces or transportation, while those with intellectual disabilities may struggle with social interactions and communication. Others, as sad as it is to say, may struggle with the sense that they fall outside the narrow, mainstream standard of beauty.

For "singles by chance" facing dim prospects and a fraught search, dating is a drag. Data from Queen Mary University of London reveals that the average heterosexual man on the dating app Tinder needs to swipe a hundred times in order to make six matches. Of those matches, only one in fifty-seven turns into an in-person meeting, and it takes five meetings with different women for something romantic or sexual to happen. It's worse in Alaska, where there are 109.2 men for every 100 women. It's also bad in countries that have gender imbalances due to sex-selective abortions, female infanticide, and unequal access to healthcare. India has a ratio of 108 men to 100 women, China has a ratio of 118 men to 100 women, and Saudi Arabia has a ratio of 137 men to 100 women. These gender imbalances translate to tens of millions of "extra" men due to tens of millions of "missing" women.

Heterosexual men have trouble finding someone who wants them. Heterosexual women are having trouble finding someone they want. You know, a guy who has a job, a car, and a nose-hair trimmer. Outside of the highly successful and high-profile male

CEOs, professional athletes, and politicians, men are lagging behind women in developed countries in astonishing fashion. Sixty percent of college students are women, both at the undergraduate and graduate level. Single women own homes at higher rates, while single men are twice as likely to still live with their parents. Men are more likely to be incarcerated and homeless. Men also struggle to stay alive, dying an average of 5.7 years earlier than women in the United States.

Given these statistics, it's hardly surprising that an increasing number of people find themselves in a state of waiting, a concept that has intrigued Kinneret Lahad, a sociologist at Tel Aviv University. Lahad has delved into the social and cultural dimensions of waiting and hoping to start a family. Through her research, she reveals that waiting is not merely an individual experience, but rather a collective phenomenon that is influenced and shaped by societal expectations.

Cultural norms often dictate the right time for relationships and family. Phrases like "act your age" and "time to grow up" reinforce these expectations and add to the stress and pressure to conform. In some countries, such as Italy, living with extended family is a cherished norm, while in others, it's the setup for basement jokes. Attitudes toward when sex should happen (or not) is also culturally influenced. For instance, the romantic comedy *The 40-Year-Old Virgin* plays with societal pressure to get laid by a certain age.

An integral aspect of Lahad's research pertains to a type of waiting unique to women: the so-called biological clock. This metaphorical clock represents a biological time constraint on a woman's ability to bear children, which is inextricably linked to societal pressure to become a parent. This metaphorical clock, with alarms set by society, keeps ticking down on a woman's ability to bear children, increasing the pressure to find a suitable partner—which explains how the book *Just Marry Him* has sold a million copies.

As Lahad aptly puts it, "You always have to fight two battles. Firstly, there is the assumption that you want children; people often ask, 'When will you have kids?' Secondly, if you don't want them, you find yourself having to defend this choice."

Melanie Notkin, author of *Savvy Auntie: The Ultimate Guide for Cool Aunts, Great-Aunts, Godmothers, and All Women Who Love Kids,* knows firsthand the psychological and emotional strain that the biological clock can impose on women who yearn for children. Melanie waited and hoped for the right guy with whom to start a family, but to no avail. In her words, "The deafening tick of the biological clock seems to drown out the sound of reason, creating a sense of panic that often leads to poor choices and emotional distress." Sounds awful.

Imagine living your life in a doctor's waiting room, at the airport between connecting flights, or riding the elevator but never going to your hotel room. Yet that is what *Someday* singles commit themselves to when they live in the liminal world of waiting for their perfect partner.

### Drawback 3: What Are You Waiting For?

The last problem with goals is they are an uncertain bet on a brighter future. Some goals, such as weight loss, when accomplished, guarantee positive outcomes. Other goals, however, are a forecast, a prediction, a hope, a dream. Unfortunately, people are notoriously bad at predicting the future or how they will feel about it when it arrives. One of my mother's sayings resonates here: "Be careful what you wish for."

Marriage is oftentimes wonderful and meaningful: There is someone for companionship, support, and a hedge against the risks of the contemporary world. Someone to split expenses.

Someone to have sex with. Someone to raise a family with. Someone to care for you when you are old. And let's not forget those tax breaks!

Riding the escalator, however, isn't a finite goal like running a marathon, writing a book, or losing weight. It's a complex interplay of factors, many of which are beyond the control of even the most privileged, well-intentioned couples. Even if the escalator aligns with a person's temperament, values, and lifestyle, there is no guarantee that their partner will remain the right fit. People change. Desires evolve. One person may crave more sex, while the other wants less—or none at all. A partner may prove untrustworthy or hinder personal growth. They may become an alcoholic. A shopaholic. A partner may put you down or beat you up. A sobering statistic from the World Health Organization reveals that about 30 percent of women and 23 percent of men globally have suffered physical and/or sexual violence from an intimate partner. Beyond a one-in-three divorce rate in the United States, researchers estimate a one-in-four rate of infidelity.

Despite these sobering facts, people are overly optimistic about their chances of marital success. A mere 5 to 10 percent of couples opt for prenuptial agreements as a safeguard.

Proponents of marriage, whether clergy, politicians, or Aunt Sally, propagate the idea that marriage makes people happier. They cite research that shows married people report being happier than single people, who, in turn, are happier than divorced people. They conclude: Get married and stay married.

I don't like Kool-Aid, but if you do, let's pause before you drink it. There are three problems with this research and reasoning.

The first problem is that this so-called life satisfaction benefit of marriage is small. The difference in happiness levels between married, single, and divorced people is tiny. The studies involve vast numbers of participants, so the difference in life satisfaction can be detected even if it is not that meaningful. In other words, knowing whether someone is married or single tells you almost nothing about how satisfied that person is with life.

To address the second problem, let's meet Bella DePaulo. That is, meet her again (you may remember her from Craig's Solo Love Letter).

On a warm, breezy day in Southern California, I made the scenic drive up Highway 101 from Los Angeles to Summerland to meet Bella, a social psychologist who has extensively researched and written about single living. In the year 2000, during a sabbatical from her professor job at the University of Virginia, she decided to take a leap of faith. She chose to pursue her passion—studying singlehood—full-time and eventually settled in this idyllic town near Santa Barbara.[2] (I know this sounds like the start of a Hallmark movie where Bella is eventually swept off her feet by a man. Spoiler alert: she isn't.) Bella's interest in the subject of singlehood began with a manila file folder labeled with the number one. This folder became the depository for her early musings and discoveries on the subject. It started with a quote from an advice column that declared, "One is a whole number."

When Bella was reviewing the research comparing the happiness of married to single people, she recognized that to show the happiness advantage, the researchers removed divorced people from the sample of married people. They were placed in a separate category. The divorced people in the sample were less happy, so by removing them, the researchers boosted the happiness of the married people. Seems sketchy to me.

It's crucial to understand that while married people may report being happier than single people, this does not necessarily mean that marriage is the cause of their happiness. The research showing a happiness advantage is correlational, which means that something else could be causing the relationship. Just because two sets of data X and Y can be linked doesn't necessarily mean that X causes Y. They could both be caused by a separate, third factor, Z, or the direction of the effect could be the other way Y causes X . That is, there could be another reason for the differences between married, single, and divorced people. As the nerds like to say, "Correlation does not imply causation."

Bella emphatically challenges people who assert a causal connection between marriage and happiness, "No study has ever shown that getting married makes people happy or healthier and no study ever will." The reason that no study ever will show a happiness advantage due to marriage is that no researcher will ever be allowed to run a study that takes bad reality television to a whole new level. Rather than to choose to marry or not, participants would be randomly assigned by the researchers to stay single, to get married, or to get married and then divorced. I call the show *Married and Divorced at First Sight*.

Even if this study could be run, there is an additional problem: You would have to consider what type of deranged people would agree to star in the ethically dubious, half-baked reality show that I just made up.

Bella advocates an alternative approach to understanding these statistics: the use of longitudinal studies. Longitudinal designs ask people their happiness at various points in time, and then compare levels of happiness before and after marriage to see if there is an increase or not. If happy married people show up as happy before they married, this would suggest a different interpretation of the data.

These studies, some of which have been conducted by hardcore economists, reveal a fascinating fact. Married people have a slight happiness advantage *before* they get married (see figure 4). Moreover, the small happiness disadvantage of people who marry and divorce is present *before* they marry. Whoa.

Longitudinal studies of life satisfaction and relationship status suggest another interpretation, one I make cautiously. People who are happy are more likely to get married and stay married. Another interpretation, one that I make even more cautiously: Happy people are just better at enduring married living.

Now, before you run from the altar, there is one way that marriage is shown to directly contribute to one's happiness: about a year before you get married and a year after. We're talking about the "honeymoon effect," a phenomenon where newlyweds experience a peak in happiness, with the highest point being the

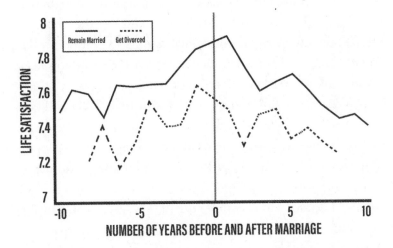

**FIGURE 4:** People who marry are happier before they marry. People who marry and divorce are slightly less happy before they marry. Notice the peak associated with the "honeymoon effect." Data from Stutzer and Frey (2003).

actual wedding day itself. The average cost of a wedding in the United States is around $30,000. That's about $40 a day for a small happiness boost—or for a fraction of the cost you could buy all the mozzarella sticks you want and the gym membership to burn them off (figure 4).

The biggest challenge of single living is not the financial costs, government policies, housing issues, or difficulty finding the right partner. The biggest challenge is how people feel about themselves for not being able to ride the escalator, or not wanting the ride in the first place.

Some people find it hard to believe that getting married does not create bliss, because when married people say they are happy, people believe them. However, when single people say they are happy, people don't.

Aunt Sally wants Thelma to be happy. The two just have different ideas of what that means. Thelma is healthy enough to do the challenging trek to Machu Picchu and has the means to afford the trip. She generously makes time to visit family and friends. She has a purpose with her new puppy. She seems like a pretty cool person. I have a crush on Thelma.

If you are a *Someday* single, living with both hope and concern, I will ask you again, what are you waiting for? Are you letting your singleness keep you from the crystal-clear waters of the Maldives, the rich history of Rome, or a stunning road trip to Yellowstone? Are you postponing a career change or a new job venture because you're waiting for the perfect partner to support your decision? Are you dreaming of your own space but putting that dream on pause in case someone special comes along? Are you waiting for a graceful partner (or any partner) to take up tango?

Imagine a world where you are not judged for being single. Imagine a world where you have the same opportunities as someone who is married. Imagine a world where you can choose the best life for you—and on your timeline.

Imagine a world built by you for you.

## SOLO LOVE LETTER

### Darlene, Change Management Consultant, Halifax, Nova Scotia, Canada

Labels can be sticky and tricky. I've often shied away from labeling myself, as I don't like feeling beholden to them. So, imagine my surprise when I discovered the *Solo* podcast a few years ago, and found myself drawn to the label "Solo."

Before "Solo," I spent the better part of twenty years soaking up all the negative rhetoric around being single. When I was thirty, I got divorced and entered the dating pool. "Successful relationships" eluded me. Internet dating only made matters worse, eroding my trust in men and my feelings of self-worth. In my forties, I simmered somewhere between acceptance of defeat and exhaustion.

I started stumbling across single-positive publications. Several "gateway" single-positive podcasts eased me into a new way of thinking about my single status. Then the *Solo* podcast came along and struck a special chord with me. What amazed me the most was that I was connecting with a concept that wasn't even fully developed! As Peter openly explored the definition of "Solo," allowing it to morph over time, I happily played along. It seems there's an underlying essence to this concept that is felt by those who "get it." It has pulled me in and made me feel a sense of relief. I've realized there are others like me. By removing the old tropes of "poor me" and "broken single" from the narrative and replacing them with single role models and research that supports singles' endeavors, the Solo movement attracts and connects like-minded people.

If you find a label that fits, wear it. There is something indescribable about having conversations with a group of people who have a shared worldview and language around an important piece of your identity, especially when most of the world is oblivious to it.

I've been through several big changes and reinventions, but this one feels the most authentic to my true self. I doubt it's a coincidence that around the same time as I discovered Solo and other single-positive narratives, I initiated personal projects that lit me up, and discovered new roles in my career that suit me better than any previously.

Keep dreaming big!

## SOLO LOVE LETTER

### Anne, retired, Massachusetts and Minnesota, USA

The elephant in the room for some singles: being undatable.

The road to a remarkable life is fraught with frustration unless one can find a path out of the forest of normative values. There are many of us who, for many reasons, are ignored or derided for being undatable.

Hemihyperplasia ruled my life until my mid-twenties, when I underwent facial surgery to correct the issue of one side of my face growing more than the other. It affected my appearance, speech, and self-esteem when other people derided me for lacking physical appeal. I never had a date in high school or college. There were few intimate relationships, and those were meaningless and unsatisfying without emotional content. Fast-forward to my early fifties, when I got a diagnosis of multiple sclerosis. At this point, I totally gave up hoping for a "normative" lifestyle.

Here's the good news that helped me find and grow a more remarkable life.

- My parents realized that I would likely have to take charge of my life as a Solo. I was taught the skills I would need to manage my own life. Housekeeping skills, the safe use of tools, and confidence to trust my decision making ensured I would be successful in running a household.
- Good grades. My ability to focus and pay attention and my stable, independent personality gave me confidence in myself to make my own choices, good or bad.
- A few good friends could enrich my life enough that I didn't need intimacy. Dislike of sexual intimacy helped me live without this physical component—I could be content, even happy, without it.
- Dogs. I have always had canine companions who adored me despite my appearance.
- Travel. Once I retired from an art teaching career, I found travel with group tours. I could go where I wanted and when I wanted (within budgetary limitations).

On reflection, I can consider my life a remarkable one, none of which would have likely happened if I'd been able to walk the "normative" path.

Nonconformity is the "norm" for Solos.

# FOUR

# A World Built for You

S weden is the singles' capital of the world, boasting one of the highest rates of singles. 40 percent of the population lives alone. In Stockholm, this figure rises to nearly 60 percent. And it can't just be because of the cheap furniture.

Thus far, I hope it is clear that society has rather recently invented and pervasively promoted a particular style of romantic relationship—one high in status and often marked by marriage. Most people pursue it at some time or another, to varying degrees of success. Because government, religious organizations, and even your family members want you to ride the escalator till you die, there are a variety of incentives and punishments designed to get you on and stay on. While there is nothing wrong with choosing that ride, it is clearly not for everyone at every moment of their life. Just as the world gave rise to marriage, it is starting to give rise to people who want to be single—whether for now or forever.

For a Solo like me, Sweden felt like the promised land. Eager to experience a country built for me, I metaphorically traded in my Stetson for an Indiana Jones–style fedora and made the solo expedition to Stockholm. This was during Sweden's midsummer festival, when residents gather to celebrate the long days and short nights of the summer solstice. They play traditional games such as *kubb, femkamp,* and *kasta hästsko,* and young women dance around the maypole with flowers in their hair. It was all rather surreal.

People's proclivity to go it alone in Sweden can be attributed to its strong welfare state and extraordinary gender equality. Universal healthcare, free education, and generous unemployment benefits abound. A high level of educational and economic opportunities means that women are not dependent on men for financial support, further enabling single living. According to Lars Trägårdh, coauthor of *The Swedish Theory of Love,* this helps Swedes to pursue lives on their own, rather than in traditional family units. He told me, "We have a social security system that gives us a sense of security, so we don't need to rely on social connections in the same way that people in other countries might."

Translation: Swedes don't need to marry to survive.

An alternative explanation for the rise of singles is that Sweden and other Scandinavian countries are individualistic to begin with—this is their natural state. Individualism focuses on personal rights, freedoms, and achievements, while collectivism emphasizes the well-being of the group through cooperation, loyalty, and social harmony. Scandinavian countries, like the United States, rank among the top ten in terms of individualism.

Individualism surely contributes to the rise of singles; however, collectivistic cultures are seeing a similar rise.

South Korea, despite its rank as the eleventh most collectivistic country, contends for the title of singles' capital of Asia. In South Korea, there is a decline in marriage and birth rates as young people opt for personal freedom over the arduous pursuit of traditional lifestyles encompassing school, work, and marriage.

Like their American counterparts, South Koreans struggle to keep up with the "Gangnam Joneses," a reference to the affluent Gangnam district of Seoul, where residents are known for ostentatious displays of wealth. The pressure to conform to traditional gender roles leads men to spend significant amounts of money on gifts, meals, and entertainment to impress their potential romantic partners. A home is often a prerequisite for marriage, but with housing prices soaring, it's difficult for young people to afford one. Even a wedding is financially draining; a survey by the Korea Wedding Culture Association indicates that the average cost of a wedding in South Korea is a staggering 100 million won (approximately US $86,000). In Seoul, this cost escalates to an eye-watering 260 million won, which is around US $224,000.

That's a lot of kimchi.

Unable to or uninterested in keeping up, an increasing number of young South Koreans are opting out of traditional culture and embracing a *honjok* lifestyle (pronounced "han-joke"), which involves engaging alone in activities—such as hiking or dining—unconcerned by what others think. The term "*honjok*" is a combination of two Korean words: "alone" and "tribe." A *honjok* chooses to be single, live alone, and spend time alone. Korean American writer Anne Babe told me how this group is typically composed of young, creative individuals, "They are really ambitious people who want to achieve their own goals and dreams." As a result, *honjoks* may not have time or energy to pursue romantic relationships, seeking to optimize their well-being.

*Honjok* culture has its own vocabulary. Examples include: 1) "*honhaeng*," or traveling alone, a trend that has been increasingly popular among young Koreans seeking independence and self-discovery; 2) "*honsho*," or shopping alone, a deviation from the typically social affair of shopping for clothes and jewelry; 3) "*honnol*," or playing alone, meaning to engage in leisure activities by oneself, such as going for a walk or visiting an arcade; and 4) "*honyeong*," or going to the movies alone, a practice that is gaining acceptance in South Korean culture. Cinemas are installing single-seat aisles. No need to fight over that armrest ever again!

"*Bihon*" is another term in South Korea prompted by women who rule out matrimony altogether. "*Bi*" means "avoid" or "escape," and "*hon*" means "marriage."

*Bihon* is an important term, because it is indicative of a trend fueling the rise of singles. According to Elyakim Kislev of Hebrew University and author of *Happy Singlehood*, the increasing empowerment of women is one of the most significant influences on women's decisions to delay marriage, remain single, or divorce a spouse.

Over the past century, women have made enormous strides fighting the patriarchy and gaining social, economic, and political rights and freedoms. American women's suffrage in 1920 was a crucial step in this process, giving women greater independence. The invention of "the pill," the 1963 Civil Rights Act and its enforcement in the 1970s, Title IX in 1972, and *Roe vs. Wade* in 1973 were all significant milestones that helped to empower women and move toward a marriage of equals.[1]

It was not until the 1970s that the United States abolished the "head and master" laws, which gave husbands complete control over their wives' property and earnings. A married woman was unable to open her own bank account, sign contracts, or make financial decisions without her husband's permission. Women could not even have credit cards in their own name in the United States until 1974. Despite progress, patriarchy persists today. Contemporary wedding ceremonies, for instance, reflect commodification of women. Stephanie Coontz, author of *Marriage, A History: How Love Conquered Marriage*, remarked,

"The tradition of giving away the bride is a poignant reminder of how deeply ingrained these ideas are in our collective consciousness."

Today, due to greater educational and economic opportunities, women in many parts of the world are beginning to outpace men and increasingly choose to forgo marriage. Since the 1960s, the labor participation rate of women has skyrocketed, reflecting a significant increase in the proportion of the working-age population actively employed or seeking employment. Men's labor participation rate has declined slightly.

Changes in social norms and access to education and career opportunities have made it more acceptable for women to prioritize their careers over starting a family. Journalist and author Ta-Nehisi Coates characterizes this trend better than I can:

> I think that human beings are pretty logical and generally savvy about identifying their interests. Despite what we've heard, women tend to be human beings and if they are less likely to marry today, it is probable that they have decided that marriage doesn't advance their interests as much as it once did.

As a global phenomenon, the rise of rebellious women is not limited to Sweden, South Korea, or the United States.

One of the most escalator-focused countries and oppressive cultures for women is India. Yet India serves as an inspiring case study for the pervasiveness of the rise and rebelliousness of women. Despite a deeply ingrained culture of family, marriage, and arranged marriage, recent demographic shifts have led to an increase in the number of single Indians, particularly young people in urban areas. Young women are pursuing higher education and career opportunities at greater rates and delaying marriage to gain more independence. Ketaki Chowkhani, an academic studying gender and singlehood, has noted how Indian women are rising up and demanding their rights. They are challenging traditional gender roles, pursuing education and career opportunities, and delaying marriage. They are also speaking out against violence and discrimination. Furthermore, there has been a shift away from arranged marriages, with younger generations placing a greater value on love and autonomy in romantic relationships. Sreemoyee Piu Kundu, a singles advocate and author of *Single Status: The Truth about Being a Single Woman in India,* told me: "India is on the cusp of not just a cultural revolution, but a sociological, demographic, economic, and sexual revolution also. This is a country where marriage and motherhood are considered the holy grail of womanhood. The singlehood or the Solo movement is integrated into these changes that our society is passing through."

Nigeria, which is projected to become the third most populous country in the world by 2050, is experiencing a cultural tug between arranged and love marriages. Either way, the culture requires an escalator ride one way or another. "The pressure to be married in Lagos is high," says Ifeoma, a twenty-something marketer. "It's like you are incomplete if you are not married." Adeola Ogunsanwo, a Nigerian writer and journalist, allegedly is responsible for a quip that is now part of Lagos lore: "Being single in Lagos is like an extreme sport that requires mental, emotional and psychological strength."

Nonetheless, there is a new force tugging on the residents, especially in cities: singlehood. In 2022, almost half of the Nigerian population ages fifteen to sixty-four was single, a rate even higher in the largest city, Lagos. Chiamaka, a thirty-two-year-old resident of Lagos, captured the Solo sentiment in an interview with Bella Naija: "Being single in Lagos can be challenging, but it's also liberating. There's a lot of pressure from society to get married and settle down, especially for women, but I'm taking my time and enjoying my freedom while I can. Lagos is a city full of opportunities, and being single allows me to take advantage of them without any restrictions."

Besides the rise of women and the cost of pursuing the "American Dream" or its cultural equivalent, there are a host of reasons why people are putting off marriage for now or forever: The rise of urban living, which makes it easier to live alone, immigration (immigrants are more likely to be single), decreasing interest in children, and inventions that make it easier to live alone (e.g., apartments and the rise of urban living more generally), to name a few.

One of the biggest factors in a global shift away from marriage is the invention of divorce and relaxation of divorce standards. One in three marriages in the United States end in divorce. In 1930, the divorce rate was one in six marriages. In 1808, it was one in twelve. The top three reasons cited for why couples divorce today are: 1) communication problems, 2) infidelity, and 3) financial issues. The bar was higher in the 1800s, when you had to prove "adultery," "desertion," "cruelness," or "habitual drunkenness." Interestingly, some researchers contend that divorce is contagious; a 2013 study in the journal *Social Forces* found that if a close friend or family member goes through a divorce, it increases a person's chance of also divorcing by 75 percent.

People recognize the risk of divorce and thus are more wary of entering long-term relationships. As sociologist Eric Klinenberg, author of *Going Solo* notes, "People are aware that marriages today are more likely to end in divorce, so they're more hesitant to enter them in the first place." It is shocking how much the government is involved in a divorce. A friend lamented to me in the middle of his divorce, "If I had known what went into getting a divorce, I would have never married in the first place."

I contend that the rise of single people (like the likelihood of divorce) is contagious. One predictor often overlooked by demographers is the presence of (happy) single people inspiring other people to stay single, or as I say: *singles beget singles.*

WHEN I WAS YOUNG, George was the only bachelor on my block. Nowadays, there are more people like him, Thelma, and the Solo community, who serve as role models for people alone yet connected. The Solo movement is gaining momentum, one friend at a time. There are more resources, too. There are books, podcasts, and online communities for singles. So, if you feel alone in your singlehood, know that you are not.

Popular culture is accelerating the spread. The earliest known love song is the "Hurrian Hymn to Nikkal," a total banger from around 1400 BCE. In recent years, however, I am seeing songs that celebrate self-love, personal growth, and individual autonomy. Now I can find playlists celebrating singlehood with songs such as Lizzo's hit "Good as Hell," Miss Eaves's "Paper Mache (Single AF)," or "Ridin' Solo" by Jason Derulo, a personal favorite.

Singles started to be represented positively in American television in 1966, with the groundbreaking sitcom *That Girl.* Starring Marlo Thomas as Ann Marie, a young single actress living in New York City, the show stands in contrast to the family shows of the day, such as *Father Knows Best* and *The Donna Reed Show.* Ann Marie was portrayed as an independent, confident, and ambitious woman who was pursuing her dreams, rather than seeking to be a wife. Other shows, such as *Living Single, Friends, Seinfeld, Sex and the City,* and *Girls,* depict independent and confident singles pursuing their dreams—albeit haphazardly on *Seinfeld.*

*The Golden Girls,* especially, has served as inspiration for women around the world to team up in retirement and take care of one another. The show, which aired from 1985 to 1992, starred Bea Arthur, Betty White, Rue McClanahan, and Estelle Getty as four indomitable women who share a home during their golden years. Each character—the sharp-tongued Dorothy, the endearing Rose, the lively Blanche, and the witty matriarch Sophia—builds a bond not defined by romance, yet as meaningful as a ride on the escalator.

The enduring popularity of *The Golden Girls* speaks to its cultural significance. The series was progressive, addressing issues such as gay rights, ageism, and women's empowerment. Moreover, it emphasized the transformative power of community, hinting at the communal living arrangements and chosen family-concepts that have become more prominent in recent times.

As people see more examples of singles in their communities, television, films, and music, these role models are likely to inspire others to embrace singlehood, leading to a future where married people become the minority. Imagine books that will be written to destigmatize married living, notably, *Partnered— Breaking the Rules in a World Built for One*

The rise of singles is not only changing the way we view marriage and family, but also influencing the economy and business landscape. Smart businesses are responding to the rise in single living by offering products and services tailored to this demographic.

Singles in Asia are ushering in a cultural shift that is significant enough for businesses to take notice. Alibaba's Singles' Day celebrated each year on November 11—11/11, get it?—reveals that there is a large and growing market for products and services tailored to singles. Since its inception in 1993 as an unofficial celebration of single living by students at Nanjing University in China, the Singles' Day holiday has become increasingly popular and incredibly profitable, with sales exceeding those of Amazon Prime Day and Black Friday combined.

In South Korea, the *honjok* trend reflects how businesses are catering to the single demographic by offering specialized products and services. Banks now offer single-household credit cards. E-commerce platforms list *honjok* as a stand-alone shopping category, selling tiny washing machines, multipurpose furniture, and one-person dishware settings. Convenience stores promote single-serving meals. Food delivery services offer takeout for one. Bars and restaurants promise solo patrons judgment-free service. Specialized karaoke joints feature individual booths.

A world is being built for you.

The comic books I read as a boy featured superheroes like Batman (Bruce Wayne), Wonder Woman (Diana Prince), Captain America (Steve Rogers), Captain Marvel (Carol Danvers), the Flash (Barry Allen), Green Lantern (Hal Jordan), Daredevil (Matt Murdock), and Black Widow (Natasha Romanoff) who had more important things to do than get married.

Unencumbered by the escalator, superheroes can dedicate time, attention, and energy into making the world a better place. Imagine Wonder Woman grabbing her lasso and striding toward her invisible jet as her husband whines, "Honey, are you going out to save the world, *again*?! We are supposed to watch Season 2 of *Married and Divorced at First Sight*."

The Pew Research Center study revealed that many singles who are forgoing dating are doing so because they have more important things to do. They may be pursuing any number of things as well: a graduate degree, a gig with the Peace Corps, moving to a new city, getting back in shape, obtaining their pilot's license, or writing a book on an ambitious deadline.

Indeed, singles often have greater flexibility and control over their lifestyle, because they are not beholden to their partner's lifestyle and familial responsibilities. They can work longer hours if they like or start a side hustle in their evenings or weekends. With greater mobility, singles can better seek out work in cities where jobs are higher paying. With greater control over their expenditures, they can lower their expenses and work less or retire early. They can travel on a budget by choosing off times for flights and vacations (e.g., no spring break trips to Disney World!). It explains why digital nomads (people who travel as they wish while working remotely), are more likely to be single; a 2018 *Fast Company* survey revealed that 74 percent of digital nomads are either single or in nontraditional relationships.

Enter Kris Marsh, a spunky Solo spitfire and author of *The Love Jones Cohort: Single and Living Alone in the Black Middle Class.* Kris and I both ended up as professors studying singlehood. Kris, who is Black, grew up in a predominantly white community, while I, a white dude, grew up in a predominantly Black community.

Kris advocates for an alternative path to success and happiness that is often overlooked: the SALA lifestyle (aka "Single and Living Alone"). Her research on SALAs reveals the opportunity of rejecting to societal expectations of marriage and family. She challenges the notion that marriage is the only path to the middle class in the African American community, especially for women. In her words, "Living alone is often looked at as a failure, particularly for women. But being single and living alone can be a strategic move toward economic stability and upward mobility. It can provide women with the opportunity to focus on their education and career, leading to greater financial independence and control over their lives." Her work stands in contrast to a basic assumption among demographers. And she has the data.

My life has unfolded in ways that my younger self, a provincial, ultra-well-behaved boy raised by a single mom, could never have imagined. People from my world do not become professors. They *do* become alcoholics, like my poor dad did.[2]

I doubt I could have pulled off my accomplishments while riding the relationship escalator. The ride requires too much time, attention, and energy from me. The challenge of graduate school was so immense that having a girlfriend seriously strained my chance to succeed. Other times in my life, when the stakes were not as high, I found the escalator kept me from doing things I wanted to do. And I wanted to do everything: write books, host theme parties, play sports, pitch TV shows, teach courses in Dubai, perform in professional comedy clubs, clown with Patch Adams, and travel on one-way tickets.

What I'm talking about, and what the *bihon* and superheroes out there understand, is opportunity costs, an important yet overlooked concept from economics: Spending money, time, energy, and attention on one thing means it cannot be spent on other things. The opportunity costs of the traditional, long-term relationship, especially a marriage, are substantial because the escalator requires maximum attention and support—a partner and kids are "everything." As evidence, single siblings are more likely than married siblings to care for an elderly parent because the married siblings already have "too much going on" with their family.

Another important concept from economics that exemplifies the opportunities of being single is optionality, which is the value of *having the ability, but not the obligation, to make choices.*

Consider a scenario in which you are contemplating purchasing a car. The opportunity cost is present when you choose one car over another, potentially missing out on the benefits the other car might have offered. Optionality, in contrast, is the value of having a range of choices among models and brands, maintaining the freedom to make a selection in the future. Optionality in romance means having the freedom to choose whether to date and, if choosing to date, the liberty to select the best partner at that moment. Opportunity cost, on the other hand, would refer to choosing one partner over another, and losing the potential benefits that could have been derived from choosing a different partner. Choosing not to go on a date in order to explore a city on your own is a matter of opportunity costs. Being able to choose where you'll explore on a solo adventure is a matter of optionality. In short, singles have greater optionality and fewer opportunity costs.

And let's not forget perhaps the ultimate perk: You don't need to deal with someone's snoring.

During my trip to Stockholm, I found myself at an outdoor café near Lake Mälaren, the Royal Palace, and City Hall. I was joined by a fellow stranger in this strange land, Yaroslava Kudrina, a Russian entrepreneur who could be mistaken for a model. Yaro, who lives in Stockholm, began schooling me on the cultural differences between Russia and Sweden.

Russians, like their supermarkets, have little optionality. Compared to Sweden, Russia has a much less developed welfare state and limited social safety net. She told me how Russian culture tells you that you can try but there is not much you can do to change your life. Notably, your family says the same thing. However, life in Sweden has lots of options—like a Swedish supermarket.

Swedes are told by their family, "You can do anything you want."

Yaro highlights a paradox: Having too many options can create pressure to make the best decisions. That pressure is absent in her native land.

Though Swedes don't necessarily rely on others for survival, this doesn't mean they lack connections. Singles around the world generally have more friends and are more involved in their communities than partnered people. Singles typically have a wide, diverse network to call on, depending on the situation: movie, museum, hike, seeking a new job, or shoulder to cry on.[3]

Trägårdh explained how Swedes balance their individual sovereignty with a need to belong in society. "Swedes are very good at being social when we want to be, but we're also very good at being asocial when we want to be." In Sweden, it's common to have a *fika*—a coffee break—with colleagues or friends. It's a way of socializing without committing to anything more than a cup of coffee.

Sweden, with its opportunity for solitude and connection, is one of the happiest countries in the world. If the data about the rise of singles is true, I feel safe to say that as more countries develop, we will be seeing a further rise of singles in places like Nigeria, India, and Saudi Arabia. As singles find themselves reflected in the world, business, religious organizations, and governments will respond by being increasingly friendly to the individual—bestowing benefits at the person- rather than the couple-level.

Here's an exciting prospect: Like the cheerful Swedes celebrating midsummer or superheroes donning their capes and masks, it's easier than ever to design your remarkable life, whether through pursuing self-improvement, embarking on

travel adventures, or savoring a cup of coffee in peaceful solitude or with a comrade. You can choose your path—go it alone,
ride the escalator, or tread a more unconventional path. More
than ever, the potential for a remarkable life is within your
reach—especially when you go Solo.

Solo is not about relationship status. It is a perspective. A state
of being.

Let's learn more about it.

## SOLO LOVE LETTER

### April, Program Manager, Arkansas, USA

**A**s a young girl, I had some Solo women who came and went in
my life. I found them fascinating, strong, and brave. I dreamed
of being an independent woman with the time and freedom.

When I was in college, I fell in love, and we quickly moved in
together. I eventually married this man who turned out to be a really
bad guy. Getting away from him took effort, planning, patience, and
perseverance. It also took strength and bravery. I harnessed the qualities I had developed growing into a woman . . . the qualities I
admired in those Solo women who graced my life as a child.

Once I was safely away from him, I started my new independent
life. I soon started dating, which was terrible since the expectation
and pressure were to find your "next husband." Good grief. So, after a
few months of that online nonsense, I deleted the apps and just
focused on me and learning, growing, developing, and improving, not
giving a single fuck about the pressures to date or couple-up. But it
was hard after a lifetime of societal pressure pushing me to find "my
other half" and the looks of pity when I'd tell people I was single and
living alone. I was constantly conflicted.

Then I found the Solo movement.

You mean there are people out there who *also* enjoy being single? You mean not only am I allowed to be happy like this, but this life provides me gifts that coupled living doesn't? You mean there's actual research that supports this? You mean I can meet and date people just for connections without the pressure and expectation that they become a committed life partner? No way!

I immersed myself in this Solo world that completely validated me. I was encouraged to live this life with the utmost pride, knowing I had opportunities my coupled friends didn't. Learning how to eat out alone, feeling proud and free to go hiking alone, and finally embracing the absolutely amazing opportunity to travel alone. My life feels so full now. But it's full of the things that empower me, complement me, the things that truly make me a brave, strong, amazing badass Solo woman. I'm more equipped now to deal with the single-ism I experience, and I have the verbiage and confidence to respond with knowledge, pride, and love for my life and myself.

My life is finally what I'd always wanted. What I'd dreamed about as a child. The Solo movement provides the foundation that I stand upon with sheer joy.

## SOLO LOVE LETTER

### Rachel, federal government employee, Jeddah, Saudi Arabia

Solo means living the life I want and choose to live. I'm not "filling time" until I get married. I'm actively, joyfully living an interesting life that fulfills me. I live overseas, I travel by myself, I create groups of friends, I deeply love my family, I develop my interests and talents, and I (hopefully) am living a remarkable life. I'm often told by married friends, "I live vicariously through you."

I was raised in a deeply religious, highly conservative home. Good girls went to college to get married. You should drop out if your husband needs you or if you get pregnant (which will "fulfill your highest and holiest calling"). I never bought that as a fulfilling way for me to live. I valued my hopes, talents, and dreams. I valued myself as a person, not a piece in someone else's game. I decided early on I wanted a master's degree (done) and a PhD (still on the list of things to do), and I wasn't going to give that up because someone else thought I should be having babies. Even so, the messaging ran deep and definitely had an effect on my psyche. I always felt a little "less than" in my church groups and knew very well that the older I got and longer I stayed single, the less value I would have.

I continued fighting this "second-class citizen" mentality by striving toward these traditional goals until I had an epiphany: *I don't want to be married.* That moment was life-changing. I didn't want to get married. They wanted me to get married. I wanted to live a remarkable, Solo life! I wanted to be independent, own my own home, travel, have an interesting career, and follow my passions.

I completely changed my mindset. I stopped trying to date. I quit logging onto dating apps. I switched careers. I stopped feeling sorry for myself as a single person. I stopped allowing others to put me down or feel sorry for me as a single person. I walked out of church meetings and other places that tried to demean my marital status. I started telling people the truth—that I am happy, fulfilled, and not interested in the relationship escalator. I'm too busy living a life I love.

# FIVE

# Single to Solo

**S**olos break the rules in a world built for two.

As we have covered, marriage is commonly accepted as the ultimate marker of personal success and fulfillment. On the flip side, singlehood can be similarly enriching.

Central to my mission is introducing the Solo mindset—a reinvention independent of relationship status. A shift to a Solo perspective will allow you to approach your (unconventional) life with confidence.

Solos aren't *Somedays*. What differentiates Solos is how they view themselves, how they feel about themselves, and how they focus on process over outcomes.

- A Solo is a whole person.
- A Solo seeks self-reliance while being connected to a community.
- A Solo questions the fictions on which the rules are based, looking past convention to design their own lives.

If you are ready to embark on a reinvention, let's delve more deeply into the three pillars of successful Solohood.

## 1. Wholehearted

Being human is not easy. Even with the incredible safety and security we have attained at the level of the individual and species, existential threats are an inescapable part of the human condition. From the inevitability of death to feeling like a speck in a vast and indifferent universe, existential threats can be debilitating or motivating. And the smarter you are, the more they loom large. So, if you wake up in the middle of the night contemplating the meaninglessness of life, congratulations!

Famous philosophers, such as Jean-Paul Sartre, Martin Heidegger, and Friedrich Nietzsche, contemplated the meaning of life and how to cope with the existential challenges of contemplating the meaning of life. I find the perspectives of Albert Camus, the French philosopher, writer, and journalist, especially relevant to the Solo transformation. His writing is also easier to read.

Camus prescribed embracing an authentic life as a one-of-a-kind being. He wrote in *The Myth of Sisyphus*, "To be yourself in a world that is constantly trying to make you something else is the greatest accomplishment." I love that quote.

An existential threat ignored by the "two become one" crowd is the notion of *singularity*. You and only you have unfettered access to your thoughts, feelings, and experiences. No matter how connected you are to family, friends, community, lovers, or even a soulmate (if you believe in soulmates), no one can know you as well as you know yourself.

Solos are complete—not half of a whole. Solos tackle the threat of aloneness by recognizing, accepting, and perhaps celebrating their singularity. Single living is not liminal, nor less than. To live a fulfilling Solo life requires a perspective shift. It's time to rewrite your story, redefine your identity, and, potentially, revamp your lifestyle. Who doesn't like a reinvention?

Social psychologist Tim Wilson's research underscores the power of personal stories in reshaping one's identity. His "story editing" technique involves revising personal narratives to reinterpret experiences and grow. For example, someone struggling with heartbreak might reframe the story from "No one will love me" to "I'm learning a lesson that will better prepare me for my future relationships." Another example: Someone struggling with their singlehood could reframe their story. "Look at the vast opportunities that I have. I can do anything I want!"

One method Wilson advocates is "expressive writing," as seen in the Love Letters to Solo you've been reading. Writing our personal stories facilitates self-discovery, personal growth, and spurs transformation. Expressive writing can be particularly useful when transitioning from single to Solo; it promotes changing narratives, especially those designed to domesticate you.

I encourage you to be vulnerable. Write your story, look at it as a Solo, and rewrite it. Let it sit for a five days or a week, come back, and responsibly, reinvent some more.

## 2. Autonomy

Throughout history and across cultures, the transition from childhood to adulthood has been marked by various rites of passage. In Jewish communities, bar and bat mitzvah ceremonies signify that boys aged thirteen and girls aged twelve become adults. At sixteen, Amish boys and girls enter *rumspringa*, a liminal period during which they can explore the outside world and choose to become an adult by committing to an Amish lifestyle. You might think this is a bunch of bull, but Ethiopian boys of the Hamar tribe engage in bull-jumping. In a ritual called *ukuli bula*, the boys who can successfully run and jump over the back of a row of bulls are allowed to become full members of the tribe and marry.

Marriage is a commonly recognized milestone to adulthood, whether symbolically executed or explicitly stated. With such a variety of markers across time and culture and such a variety of modern walks of life, what standard should mark the transition to adulthood? Reaching a particular age? Jumping over bulls? Tying the knot?

Iris Schneider, a behavioral scientist, proud Solo, and frequent guest on my podcast, has a simple yet profound answer for what makes someone an adult: "The difference between an adult and a child is that an adult is a good parent to themselves."

Parents educate their children, provide a moral compass, and foster social skills. However, the most critical responsibilities of parents are to provide:

- *Basic needs*: offer food, clothing, and shelter, ensuring the child's physical well-being.
- *Safety*: create a healthy, secure environment.
- *Emotional support*: love the child and encourage growth.

To fail at these responsibilities is to fail as a parent.

Solos cultivate self-sufficiency. If you can provide for your own basic needs, safety, and security, and be able to soothe and love yourself, then congratulations. You are an adult.

The traditional nuclear family, with its strict gender roles, potential for isolation, and the ever-present risk of divorce, is a useful case study for the value of self-sufficiency within a relationship.

Throughout much of the history of marriage, a wife was traded from one "parent" to another, as her husband became responsible to provide for her. Nowadays, the reverse is, sadly, too often true. I have witnessed too many husbands unable to function without a wife. His wife feeds him, dresses him, fills his social calendar, and is his sole source of emotional support. Without her, he struggles with basic tasks. Although married and perhaps a parent, he is a child by the Solo definition of adulthood. A child who is in loads of trouble if his wife divorces him, becomes disabled, or dies.

When psychologist Dan Kiley coined the term "Peter Pan Syndrome" in 1983, he also introduced the term "Wendy Syndrome" to describe women who act like mothers toward their partners. Humbelina Robles, a researcher from the University of Granada, contends that Wendy plays an essential role in Peter Pan's life. She takes care of everything that Peter Pan neglects, which allows Peter Pan to remain in his childlike state. Wendy makes all the decisions and takes on the responsibilities of her partner, thus justifying his unreliability.

Like the airplane safety briefing, "Put on your own oxygen mask first before helping others." A Solo life is one that prioritizes your well-being and then cultivates connections with others. Self-sufficiency makes close connections a welcome option rather than a desperate necessity. Adding value rather than filling a void.

Soloness is independent of relationship status. Solos can partner and partner well. Fostering autonomy can mitigate the risk of codependence and contribute to a more stable, resilient, and fulfilling interdependent partnership. Autonomy within a relationship reduces dependence, allowing for a more balanced and equitable distribution of responsibilities. The overall burden on any one person is diminished. Partners want each other rather than need each other. Moreover, in the case of divorce, disability, or death, the other person can step up as needed.

Later in the book, I'll show you how to establish a foundation of well-being that supports autonomy and independence. In the meantime, let's continue the writing task. If you are considering transitioning to Solo, ask:

- Am I aggressively pursuing financial security?
- Am I taking good care of my physical and mental health?
- Am I cultivating a support system outside of romantic partnerships?

### 3. Unapologetically Unconventional

Camus urged people to rebel against injustice and oppressive systems of power. In his book *The Rebel*, he wrote, "The only way to deal with an unfree world is to become so absolutely free that your very existence is an act of rebellion." Another banger of a quote by Camus.

Solos recognize that what is good for society is not always good for the individual. For example, the expectation that people should conform to traditional gender roles is limiting. When men are not allowed to be vulnerable, their mental health suffers. (Besides, I like a good cry.) When women are forced to prioritize caregiving over career, their opportunities are diminished.

Human domestication, by way of arbitrary and slowly changing fictions, presents too narrow a path to a good life. In reality, there are many ways to live remarkably. Some people work to live. Others live to work. Some people praise God. Some people sleep in on Sunday. Some students can sit still and sit quietly. The class clown says, "No thanks."

Thinking unconventionally allows Solos to better customize their relationships without relying on ill-suited norms. They pause and assess rather than defaulting in. Beyond questioning the norms that govern romantic relationships, Solos question "the rules," and they take it one step further. As Pablo Picasso would say, "Learn the rules like a professional, so that you can break them like an artist."

In the same way that Solos do not default into pursuing relationships to solve their problems, Solos are comfortable with values and lifestyles that may diverge from the dominant culture. For example, as nonconformists, Solos are more likely to have anti-consumerist attitudes—perhaps skipping the big, expensive wedding should they marry. They might also forgo a large house as expected by societal norms, choosing smaller, minimalist living spaces. They are comfortable challenging gender roles; for example, a woman might choose to be the breadwinner while her partner stays at home to care for children.

If you want to shift from single to Solo, recognize the pervasiveness of arbitrary, even inappropriate, fictions so you can break them with purpose (and perhaps panache). Get honest with yourself about what matters most to you. Identify your core values, beliefs, and lifestyle, independent of what others think. Then, practice overcoming default thinking by pausing, noticing, and deciding whether to follow the norm or forge your own path.

## PETE, MEET PETER

My evolution as a Solo came in three stages—and I needed to change my name to make it stick.

Wholeheartedness occurred in my late thirties after the breakup with the fashionista (for more, see "Your Guide"). It took profound heartbreak for me to recognize that I was complete and unique. Singular.

My self-reliance and ability to parent myself occurred much earlier. My mom had two kids in elementary school when she divorced my dad. With full custody and little money, she fed us with government peanut butter, milk powder, and food stamps. (Government peanut butter tastes exactly like you imagine.) At thirteen, I began working as a stock boy at the local Acme market in order to buy my school clothes. I soon learned not to mix whites and colors in the laundry, to keep my tighty whities white.

I left home at eighteen and put myself through college at Rutgers University (it was easier back then). Loving the freedom, fun, and intellectual stimulation of university life, I sucked the marrow out of those four years. As graduation approached, I considered my prospects. I could get a Jersey job, meet a Jersey girl, have Jersey kids, buy a Jersey house, and vacation at the Jersey Shore.

Sorry, Snooki. Instead, I moved to Southern California to work at UC Santa Barbara, then Ohio for grad school at Ohio State, back to Jersey for a post-doc at Princeton, and on to my current home at the foot of the Rocky Mountains (cue John Denver). Along the way, I managed to travel the world from Peru to Poland to Palestine, giving talks to companies and teaching at universities around the world. I could do all this by forgoing a family, keeping my expenses low, and saying yes to opportunities that were more fun and less exhausting than changing diapers in the middle of the night.

I am proud to be a good parent to myself. I can cook my own meals, keep a tidy home (perhaps too tidy), have ambitious plans to retire early, and take care of my health (for a recent colon cancer screening, I shat in a box and mailed it to a lab). Like many Solos, I have a diverse array of close friends and professional connections with people from age twenty-one to seventy-seven.

My independence and self-sufficiency staved off codependence in my relationships. One particularly sweet girlfriend's not-so-sweet mother told her, "He doesn't need you." This comment was not meant as a compliment.

The last step in my Soloness, embracing unconventionality, didn't take hold till I was on the other side of fifty.

Throughout my whole life, family, friends, teachers, students, bosses, coworkers, and coaches called me Pete. As a little boy, "Pete" learned to follow the rules—and follow them well. It kept me in my mother's good graces, yet I resented the capricious nature of the rules and her enforcement. As I entered adulthood, I kept at it. Pete kept doing all the right things, like a good little boy, and was rewarded for it. I viewed life, especially my academic life, as a train trip with stops—milestones and achievements—along the way. Working tirelessly not to get kicked off the train, Pete followed the rules for a traditional, successful life: earned multiple degrees, worked long hours in the lab, and purchased a home.

Check. Check. Check.

To stop being the good little boy, "Pete" needed therapy, long talks with friends, hours of journaling, hundreds of podcast episodes, and Solo psilocybin trips in the Joshua Tree desert. Talking about my problems helped me to process them and to feel less alone. Journaling helped me to track my progress and to identify patterns in my behavior. Mushrooms made it all stick.

The final step of my Solo transformation happened as I made a purposeful symbolic change to become "Peter." Besides the psychological and emotional transformation, there was a physical transformation—a makeover of sorts—including growing my beard and adding a Stetson cowboy hat to my fashion repertoire.

It took me nearly five decades to transition from Pete to Peter. I no longer think there is something wrong with me for wanting an unconventional, remarkable life. I started seeing life as a voyage, where I could choose the ports I wanted to visit. I am here to offer my guidance for your own transformation to Solo.

Solos are not martyrs. As my wise friend Jeff Leitner likes to remind me, "You can either follow the rules and be happy or break the rules and be happy. You cannot break the rules and be unhappy when you are punished." Jeff is so right. Remind yourself, "I chose this."

The good news is that you will not be punished for breaking the rules as often as you might expect. There is a psychological phenomenon called the *spotlight effect*. People think that others are noticing them much more than they actually are. Instead, everyone is worried about what other people think of them and therefore are too distracted to care much about what others are doing. In short, you're so vain that you probably think this paragraph is about you.

Researchers at Cornell University in 2000 asked college students to put on a T-shirt bearing a large, unflattering image of Barry Manilow. While grandma likes Manilow, these students thought the T-shirt was decidedly uncool. One at a time, the T-shirt wearers joined a group of peers. Afterward, the students wearing the T-shirt were asked to estimate how many of their peers noticed who was on the T-shirt. On average, the persons wearing the embarrassing T-shirt guessed that about twice the number of peers noticed as actually did.

Moreover, when others enforce social norms, they tend to do so through disapproval: side glances, furrowed brows, maybe a snarky comment. You can handle this. For years, social media has been training you to be judged by strangers who don't really care about you.

Finally, you may read this and wonder: *Will I be making the world worse off? Am I disappointing my parents? My friends? My boss? Peter, are you turning me into a monster?*

Check the guardrails. Do no harm. Obtain consent when appropriate. Remember, the people trying to get you to behave the way they want and not the way you want are putting their happiness in front of yours. They are adults and can handle the disappointment They have been well trained, disapprovingly scrolling through social media.

I struggle with bending or breaking the rules even when I know they are arbitrary and don't suit me. Even with the name change, therapy, mushroom trips, and fashion makeover, I sometimes regress. I toss and turn in the middle of the night. I stress out. I worry about what other people think. But I do so less than before. Don't get discouraged if you don't see results immediately.

The solution is to seek freedom in your mind.

Victor Frankl was an Austrian psychiatrist and author of *Man's Search for Meaning*—one of the most important books ever written. Frankl was a Holocaust survivor and explores finding mental freedom in the most oppressive, tragic circumstances: as a prisoner in a Nazi concentration camp. He was sent first to Theresienstadt, a Nazi-controlled way station, and then to Auschwitz.

Frankl contends that one's ability to choose one's attitude in any given situation is the ultimate freedom. Regardless of your objective circumstance, seek to free yourself within. He writes: "Between stimulus and response there is a space. In that space is our power to choose our response. In our response lies our growth and our freedom."

Solo living is about mindset more than relationship status. You get to chart your own voyage and revel in defying convention. So, partner up or not. Just remain unapologetic about who you are. Be a good parent to yourself. Celebrate your singularity. When you do that, you are no longer defined by your relationship status.

You are a Solo.

## SOLO LOVE LETTER

### Jessalyn, Business Strategy Advisor,
### Serial Migrant Probably Somewhere in Italy

I grew up in the Disney-Princess-era, which led me to spend my teens and twenties on the hunt for my "one true love" who would serve all of my needs for the rest of time. Failure after failure, I wondered when it would be my turn? When I finally met "the one" in my early thirties, we boarded the relationship escalator and let it carry us along its default social template for heterosexual monogamy. Then, in 2017, even though I had everything that society told me that I should want and deserved, I had my realization that this template was not serving my soul. I shifted to living a Solo life by uncoupling from my partner to (successfully) preserve our meaningful and loving friendship.

Today, living Solo means that I live by myself with my two cats, and my dating profile says, "not your future girlfriend, not your future wife." I travel the world, innovate solutions to society's problems, eat ice cream for breakfast when I feel like it, never get in arguments about money with my two cats, and spend time building on existing and new relationships.

I am never questioned about my decisions unless it's by complete strangers who suggest perhaps I just haven't yet met the right one. I have been very lucky to have supportive friends and family through this journey. I find that in the years since my Solo journey began, my relationships tend to express their appreciation to me with precise, itemized gratitude (meaning, with examples) in a more free-form way than before. My friends comfortably and lovingly step into their enhanced importance in my life because they know that I'm not resting back on some "default person" in case they can't come through for me in a time of need.

One of the most profound moments of my Solo journey was stepping into the concept of living a remarkable life. This came to me after I moved to Europe from the United States in 2017 and had the realization: *If finding my one true love and living happily ever after isn't the reason for existing, then what is?* I realized that I needed to rediscover the purpose of life when that escalator was no longer it. "I want to be someone who gave more than I took" is my new purpose, and how I execute on that purpose changes organically with time and circumstances.

## SOLO LOVE LETTER

### Alex (she/her), Curriculum Coordinator, Melbourne, Australia

My journey to identifying as Solo began unexpectedly. I live in Melbourne, Australia. During the pandemic, my city had the rare privilege of being one of the most locked-down cities in the world. It was about halfway through one of the many lockdowns when my husband and best friend of twenty-five years said these words, "I can't do this anymore," and moved out of our family home and . . . in with his girlfriend.

Wait, what? What just happened? I did all the right things. I was a dutiful wife and mother . . . I rode the escalator.

I was devastated, but as it turns out—he did me a favor.

Our life was okay. We did the things. We lived the life. We were okay. It wasn't until he left that I realized that life could be more than okay. Life could be exceptional.

That's not to say I got to that point right away. If I'm honest, I sat on the couch, cried, and ate chocolate for about twelve months. It was like zero gravity had taken me off the relationship escalator, and I was just floating untethered in space. . . . Who was I without being a wife? What do I do now? What about the future I had mapped out? And then a single female colleague said to me, "I have been listening to this podcast; I think you might like it—it's called *Solo*."

Oh. My. Goodness!!!! What a revelation.

Going Solo has turn my life around.

From the intro—the single person's guide to living a remarkable life. . . . A remarkable life. Hmm, that sounds more like it. I can be unapologetically unattached?! I can do what I want, when I want? I can eat, sleep, read, create, dream, go, think, be, and do what I want, when I want. . . . My whole perception flipped, and instead of being untethered, I had my feet firmly planted on the ground. In fact, it was like I arrived into my own body, into my true self, for the first time.

I couldn't believe I hadn't thought of this sooner. I didn't have to be apologetic about being single. I could celebrate, rejoice! For the first time in a *very long* time, I felt free to be myself.

Well-meaning friends say to me "You'll find someone," and I think, *Hell no!*

I'm having the time of my life, living my truth and am *so* happy!

# SIX

# Just May

On a warm midsummer day during my Indiana Jones–style expedition to Stockholm, I visited Haymarket, a bustling square in Stockholm's Norrmalm district. With the sun high in the sky, I sat at a charming outdoor café where I met Hannah, an equally charming thirty-one-year-old change management worker at a tool company. We sipped cappuccinos and talked about her life in the singles capital of the world.

The conversation drifted toward dating and relationships among thirty-something Swedes. Like her friends, Hannah spends much of her time and energy building her career, hanging with friends, working out, and traveling throughout Europe and beyond. She dates and suspects she will eventually have a family, but she expressed her gratitude for not being in a long-term relationship. She was all very nonchalant about it.

Like many of her fellow Swedes, Hannah is a *Just May*.

*Someday* singles are waiting and hoping—sometimes hopelessly—to find an escalator partner. *Just Mays* are Solos open to riding the escalator but not waiting around for the ride. They do not feel incomplete. They seek to solve their own problems and are open to many paths to a remarkable life. They embrace exploration, flexibility, and personal growth as they navigate their dating journey.

The Solo movement has a big tent. Unlike the escalator that has room for only one type of couple in one type of relationship, the Solo community makes space and encourages all types of proud singles from *Just Mays* to *No Ways* to *New Ways* (but more on those later) reflecting just how varied and diverse the world's single population is.

*Just Mays* are hopeful romantics; they live, date, and partner differently than their *Someday* brothers and sisters. Because a relationship is one desire of many—not a need.

## *JUST MAYS* LIVE DIFFERENTLY

Kristin Newman, a writer and producer, followed a typical Hollywood production cycle: Grind on a show for months on end and then take a much-needed vacation once production wraps. Her funny, insightful memoir, *What I Was Doing While You Were Breeding*, opens with a captivating confession: "I am not a bad girl in the United States of America."

Newman introduces the reader to her adventurous alter ego, "Kristin Adjacent," and presents her compelling journey through her twenties and thirties, where she experiences liberation while traveling abroad, in contrast to her restrained life stateside. Newman's narrative offers a testament to the adventurous spirit of the *Just May* Solo lifestyle.

Much like her fellow *Just Mays*, Newman was not waiting for life to happen—she zealously pursued it. Embodying the Solo philosophy, she challenged conventional norms, setting off on quests for enriching experiences that fostered personal development and excitement. She embraced spontaneity, was open to connections, and led a life less ordinary. Assuming the persona of her alter ego, Newman traversed the globe from the sun-drenched beaches of Brazil to Russia's picturesque domes set against a winter wonderland. Her book tells the tales of her poignant—and occasionally naughty—connections with locals and travelers alike. She observed, "This Kristin-Adjacent creature . . . she's less judgmental, more open, a little softer."

With her Solo identity deeply ingrained, Newman eventually navigated a new path to marriage and motherhood. While she cherished her adventures in singlehood, she transferred her zest into parenting. Reflecting on her transition, she reveals, "I had learned that as boring as I found parents [to be] when I was single and childless, having a child is the most interesting thing I've ever done by a long shot. It turns out it's not boring. It's just boring to hear parents talk about their children."

I witnessed my friend Megan blossom into a *Just May*, as she went from hopelessly wanting to ride the escalator to not waiting around. I met Megan, an elementary school teacher, at Orange Theory—a fitness class where participants rotate among tread-mill runs, rowing machines, and HIIT-style floor exercises (that's HIIT—high intensity interval training). I felt like I was in a com-mercial for the gym, as I watched her and her sister smile, laugh, and dance their way from station to station. I was drawn to Megan's energy and tremendous smile. We chatted between sets on the rower, and, old-school style, I asked for her number. We dated briefly and transitioned to being friends (without bene-fits). Her choice. Not mine.

Smart, vivacious, stable, with traditional sensibilities, Megan has "it." I suspected she would eventually ride the escalator, and as a *Someday* single, so did she. However, with time, I saw her start to question convention. She took a sabbatical from her teaching job to teach in Copenhagen (another haven for singles) and go on adventures through Europe. We reconnected as part of a group Solo trip I was hosting in Barcelona.[1] Megan told me how the escalator was increasingly optional for her. Nevertheless, I was not surprised when she got engaged a couple years later. I suspect her husband is thrilled by the prospects of a life with this gem of a person. As evidence of her Soloness, the couple eloped in their backyard.

## JUST MAYS DATE DIFFERENTLY

Twenty-five-year-old Sasha Cagen was single and ready to mingle at a Brooklyn New Year's Eve party. As the ball dropped, she looked around the room for someone to kiss and found no one. She also found no one else was kissing either. She had the epiphany, "I'm not the only one."

One year and seven hundred words later, she started a movement. Her essay "The Quirkyalone: Celebrating Single Life," resonated with thousands of women who want a fulfilling life that *might* include a romantic relationship. She told me, "Quirkyalone is really about not settling for a relationship that doesn't feel right to you."

Quirkyalones aren't buying the book *Just Marry Him*.

Cagen encouraged her Quirkyalone sisters not to wait around: embrace solitude, foster deep friendships, practice self-care, seek travel and adventure, and express creativity. Quirkyalones pursue personal fulfillment and growth while cherishing independence. Not settling in love or life. Quirkyalones are comfortable being single but are romantics at heart.

While some *Just Mays* are not willing to settle, others are letting go of their pursuit of perfection. For them, dating no longer mirrors an interview process designed to find the ultimate growth marriage, a process in which a single weakness can stop a relationship in its tracks.

As a recovering perfectionist and goals addict, I am learning not to let perfection be the enemy of good. I understand about the relentless pursuit of perfection. Goals have played a pivotal role in shaping my success. With near laser focus, I can work relentlessly day after day, month after month, year after year, to accomplish a task. It is why I am often simultaneously energized and exhausted. Nowadays, rather than living in the shadow of tomorrow, I find myself reevaluating this approach, departing from a fixation on future perfection and focusing instead on process.

Some people would classify *Sex and the City*'s Carrie Bradshaw a *Someday* single, because she's so relationship oriented (she writes a relationship column, after all). I suggest instead that she is a *Just May*. Despite the show's lengthy relationship arc with Mr. Big, Carrie often dates people whom she knows will not lead to marriage. Unlike her friend Charlotte, who cuts ties with a man when she realizes he isn't marriage material, Carrie dates for fun, excitement, or pure sociological research. Her open-mindedness (and equally open-minded fashion choices) lead her to a range of rich experiences (after all, she has a deadline for her relationship column). As Carrie says: "Dating is like trying on clothes. You don't know if it's going to fit until you try it on."

*Just Mays'* openness, comfort, and confidence make them more appealing to go out with. They're not conducting an interview designed to find a soulmate. You know what is a major turnoff when you are meeting someone? Being interviewed on a first date about your potential fit as a life partner. *Just Mays* make dating an opportunity for self-discovery and growth, rather than a means to an end. Kinneret Lahad calls this "non-waiting."

Pre-Solo, I naïvely thought the right person "to complete me" was an extroverted Sporty Spice type—essentially my doppelgänger in feminine form. When I went Solo, I threw out my checklist approach and started using my feelings to choose to see someone again. Dating became more fun, and I met all sorts of wonderful women who were often artsy and introverted partners—sometimes for a few dates or friends with benefits for years.

The *Just May* approach is counterintuitive to the *Somedays*, who are hopelessly pining away, the picture of desperation. *Just Mays* are too busy living remarkably to be desperate. Instead of engaging in activities to make themselves attractive to others, they concentrate on self-improvement for personal fulfillment. For instance, they don't get fit merely to catch someone's eye; they exercise because it is good for them. The same goes for fashion choices. Rather than dressing up purely to impress, *Just Mays* choose outfits that make them feel confident and happy in their own skin. *Just Mays* travel for fun and fulfillment, not to show off Machu Picchu in their dating profile.

By dating differently, *Just Mays* become more attractive to others. Their rich and diverse experiences make them more engaging and intriguing partners, like Kristin Newman, who have stories to tell and wisdom to share. Their authenticity shines through as they are not trying to fit into a mold to please someone else. This genuineness is refreshing in a dating landscape with so many posers.

Going Solo is romantically and sexually expansive.

## *JUST MAYS* PARTNER DIFFERENTLY

Not all singles are Solo—and not all Solos are single.

Solos don't stop being Solo if they ride the escalator. The desire for independence fosters coordination in Solo partnerships. If *Just May* Solos decide to partner up and settle down, they remain Solos—whole, autonomous, and free to be themselves. You know, like Oprah.

The sneaky thing about *Just Mays* is that their success as singles tends to carry over into relationship success. Because of their comfort with independence, coordination is an overarching theme in Solo partnerships. I have a Solo friend who met a man when she was single. He asked her if she had plans that Friday, and she told him that she was going to the movies alone. His response, "Do you want somebody to go to the movies alone with you?" That played well. They are now married with a kid.

Most single people I know are familiar with being tossed aside when a friend becomes infatuated with a new love interest—only to have the friend return when the relationship ends and act as if nothing happened. My working label for this phenomena: friendship fade and the breakup boomerang.

If you are aghast, thinking, *I would never do that!* Great. You may already be a Solo—or at least well on your way.

*Just Mays* make loyal friends. Carrie Bradshaw's best friend on *Sex and the City* is Miranda, who is also a *Just May*. Miranda is a highly successful, high-powered lawyer who went to Harvard Law School. Sometimes her career success is a hindrance to her dating; men are intimidated by her. But regardless of how things are going romantically, the two friends remain close and connected. *Sex and the City* would not work if the characters disappeared every time a love interest came along.

Partnered Solos sometimes bend the rules of the escalator. Perhaps they don't live with their partner. Or maybe they just like to go to the movies alone. Going Solo can strengthen a relationship; being whole, self-reliant, and unconventional is sexy. Solos are more appealing partners. They have more confidence. They are not needy. They are better at shaping life rather than being shaped by it. Coordination is an overarching theme.

*Just Mays* also know how to keep things sexy.

Esther Perel, the Belgian psychotherapist and relationship expert, is best known for her book *Mating in Captivity: Unlocking Erotic Intelligence.* She addresses a risk of riding the escalator: the end of good sex. It's a paradox: The presence of security and predictability, which keeps things stable, conflicts with the need for novelty and excitement, which keeps things hot.

Perel presents advice about how to keep things steamy. Balancing connection and autonomy, partners maintain intimacy and eroticism. One prescription, maintaining individuality, is the hallmark of the Solo. Partners should pursue separate interests, hobbies, and goals, allowing each person to evolve independently, keeping the relationship fresh and novel. Having one's own personal space and spending time apart can also create a healthy sense of longing and anticipation, fostering desire. Cultivating separate friendships and social networks can also benefit partners' lives by providing fresh perspectives and experiences. Perel also suggests regulating self-disclosure. Sharing every thought and feeling can erode the intrigue that fuels passion. As she says, "When two people become one, we say they are joined together, fused. But it is in the space between them that the erotic lies."

## ARE YOU A *JUST MAY*?

As you contemplate the *Just May* way, you might question your own need for an escalator ride.

As you rethink, you may consider conducting a thorough self-audit. Look at your motivations beyond societal expectations and norms to uncover your true desires. Reflect on Megan's journey: She questioned the default, which opened doors to new travels and growth.

A fundamental aspect of the *Just May* philosophy is the zest to embrace life in the present moment. No more waiting around for life to happen. I admire Kristin "Adjacent" Newman's passion, vibrancy, independent of relationship status. Open yourself to pursue your interests, chase your curiosities. Sasha Cagan didn't become an author to impress others. She did it because she had seven hundred words inside her that she needed to share with her Quirkyalone sisters.

As you journey, let the importance of friendships and family relationships remain paramount. Consider letting go of your dating checklist. Pursue a delicate balance between connection and autonomy within relationships. Retaining your individual identity fuels the passion that keeps relationships thriving.

### SOLO LOVE LETTER

**Kriss, Educator/Coach/Consultant, Portland, Oregon, USA**

I wanted, I tried, I realized, I blossomed.

I spent a good portion of my life badly wanting a partner. I was on a quest to find a person, my person, "the" person. Everyone was expecting it. Growing up, I was expected to marry and have kids more than anything else.

I am the kind of person who makes things happen. I problem-solve, and so that was my journey when "relationship" felt like my destination. I was convinced that once I found that partner, I'd arrive at some state of happiness that I couldn't ever have while single.

And so, on this desperation-fueled journey, I tried all the things. I did personal ads of the early '90s. No photos, just show up to meet a stranger at a Barnes & Noble. One of the dates, I picked up at her house! Yes, that's right, I also dated women after a lifetime of dating men. I wasn't about to count out half the population in my quest. I did some speed dating, which was . . . interesting. I started my own Singles Meet-up Group so I could be in charge of the events. I moved across the country to Montana and worked on a trail crew, where the men live and work. Oh, and I did all the apps and online dating sites multiple times, seeking men, women, pansexuals, bisexuals, nonbinary, and so on. I read books with titles like *Calling in the One* and followed the instructions. I manifested, vision boarded, and did a couple tarot card/psychic readings with predictions that left me hanging. I did a stint in the ENM/poly (ethical nonmonogamy and polyamory) world and met very interesting people and had some great sex. Along the way, I had a relationship or two and tried to stay together. But nope.

As my last relationship ended, I found myself waking up to the realization that I didn't want to wait any longer to craft the life I wanted. I realized that what I thought I wanted, I no longer wanted! I began to realize that "relationship" was not the destination. I thought, *There's definitely another way.* I started taking stock in what made me happy today and yesterday and what was likely to bring happiness tomorrow. I started noticing all the things that conjured joy. This is when the Solo community came into my life, and I felt a deep sense of relief and belonging. I found myself nodding while listening to other viewpoints outside the coupled narrative. I felt empowered and finally felt less alone, with a sense of purpose to love myself fully. I made the conscious shift from single to Solo.

Finally, I could enjoy the journey without projecting forward from a place of desperation. I could be me, fully, and find a plethora of ways to fill my cup. I started noticing and reveling in the remarkable life I already had. I continued to craft that remarkable life with abandon and a multitude of options that includes a fabulous community, deepening friendships, travel, solitude, creativity, learning, friends with benefits and benefits without friendship, love, and full on blossoming.

What's next? Will I couple again? Maybe. I get to choose and design the path. It could happen and it could not; I still get to live a remarkable life of my own choosing either way. Romantic relationships will probably happen along the way, but they are no longer the destination, and they will be by design, rather than dictated by convention. That is true freedom, and I'm here for it.

## SOLO LOVE LETTER

### Mary Delia, Author of *Enjoy Your Solo*, Ft. Lauderdale, Florida, USA

In my twenties and thirties, "finding someone" was a task that I gave a lot of time and energy to without much success. I had jobs, adventures, an active social life, a big personality, and all kinds of friends. Still, I never got it together with a partner to ride the relationship escalator. At the time, I had feelings of being unworthy and being unchosen. Dating was not in my skill set, and my insecurity with intimacy and the opposite sex was high.

At the same time, I was hired as the lead travel director for a company called Singles Travel International. I took people who were single on vacation. I saw all kinds of singles having all kinds of fun. Widows who had long planned to see Venice with their spouse rode the gondola with new friends instead.

I had a blast. I discovered the "cruisemance," a romance that lasts the length of the cruise. My single guests and I had once-in-a-lifetime travel experiences over and over again with not a couple in sight.

What if you only had 365 days until your perfect partner appeared? What would you be sure to do in your last year being single? Go do lots of whatever that is! When you think about *forever* with someone, what will you miss about being single? Go do lots of whatever that is! Never compare the best of being in a couple with the worst of being single. Never compare anything about being single with an idealized version of being a couple. The energy you are spending on seeking or recovering from a love relationship is far better spent on building a Solo life you love. The Solo life is one-size-fits-one, built by and for *you*. There's always time for love . . . but the Solo season in your life could be fleeting!

# SEVEN

# No Way

S olo is the punk rock of lifestyles. And I know who the lead singer is.

Henry Rollins, the musician, actor, writer, and spoken word artist, brims with confidence and creativity. In the early 1980s, twenty-year-old Rollins left his mundane job as a manager at Häagen-Dazs for the remarkable, chaotic world of punk rock, leading the influential band Black Flag. A dynamic force, Rollins epitomizes the Solo mindset of completeness, independence, and unconventional thinking.

From punk rock singer to polymath, Rollins embodies the idea of living on one's own terms. Despite his intense onstage persona, he is a self-described loner who enjoys spending time alone to recharge and reflect. Rollins publicly professes his love for solitude, attributing it as the source of peace and clarity in his otherwise tumultuous world. As he puts it, "I was always drawn to the idea of being alone. I liked that sense of being self-sufficient." His solitude allows him to focus on his creative work, free from distractions and the pressures of social interaction, including romantic ones. He once told a woman who was interested in dating him, "Listen, ma'am, there's no way you wanna be with me. . . . You think you do, but you don't. I am so consumed by what I do, and what I do is everything to me, and I don't have time for anything else."

Rollins is no homebody. He travels solo to the most dangerous places in the world. He toured North Korea in 2013. He has visited Afghanistan multiple times, including during periods of intense conflict and instability. He has performed for US troops in Iraq, and has traveled extensively in Africa, including countries plagued by conflict (Somalia), humanitarian crises (South Sudan), and war (Democratic Republic of Congo). If he were on the escalator, these are the kinds of places Rollins might have had a hard time getting "approval" for.

Henry Rollins and other *No Way* Solos are the antithesis of *Somedays*. Despite societal pressures and the perceived status and benefits of marriage, they find fulfillment in singlehood, often preferring it to any form of romantic relationship. They are a big group, too. I keep coming back to the remarkable Pew Research Center stat that 50 percent of single adults in the United States are currently not dating casually, nor seeking a long-term romantic partner.

Does that stat make you wonder why so many singles are unapologetically unattached? It starts to make sense when you consider the vast array of reasons, relationship-related and not, why people take a temporary or permanent break from dating: concentrating on personal growth, focusing on career development, recovering from a breakup, healing emotionally, addressing past trauma, pursuing educational opportunities, social activism, traveling, strengthening friendships and family bonds, caring for an aging parent, seeking financial security, building a business, saving money, exploring new hobbies, relocating, improving health and wellness, or embracing solitude, self-reflection, spiritual pursuits, and writing lists.

Delving further into the Pew Research Center data, the most common reasons people have opted out of dating are positive in nature. Nearly half of the respondents (47 percent) believe they "have more important priorities right now."

Just ask Susan B. Anthony, the suffragist, abolitionist, and women's rights activist. Anthony believed that women should have the freedom to pursue their own interests and goals, and that marriage should not be the only path available to them, stating, "I never felt I could give up my life of freedom to become a man's housekeeper. When I was young, if a girl married poor, she became a housekeeper and a drudge. If she married wealthy, she became a pet and a doll. I thought I would have none of either."

Recognizing the constraints that marriage could place on her ambitions, Anthony focused her efforts first on the temperance movement, which advocated for the prohibition of alcohol, and later the abolitionist movement, which sought to end slavery. In 1851, she teamed up with fellow activist Elizabeth Cady Stanton—who happened to be married with seven children—to advance women's rights, including the right to vote. The women formed a lifelong partnership and collaboration. Anthony excelled in oratory, while Stanton was a formidable writer, Stanton quipped. "I forged the thunderbolts, and she fired them."

Anthony didn't just speak; she acted. In a daring act of civil disobedience, she cast a vote in the presidential election, an act then illegal for women, and was promptly arrested in 1872. She refused to pay the $100 fine (equivalent to about $2,500 today). Unfortunately, Anthony did not live to see the fruition of her efforts. She passed away in 1906, fourteen years before the passage of the Nineteenth Amendment to the Constitution, which gave women the right to vote.

Like Susan B. Anthony, some *No Way* Solos choose this path "for now" to achieve specific goals, such as going through medical school or fighting addiction.

Other *No Ways* are lifelong singles who innately know that they are not interested in marriage or traditional coupling. Indeed, the next most popular response to the Pew Research Center was the 44 percent who said they "just like being single." Younger singles are more inclined to prioritize other aspects of life, while older singles predominantly relish the state of being single. These people are living their best lives as singles.

In her book *Single at Heart,* Bella DePaulo calls this group "single at heart." Singles at heart cherish their independence, enjoy solitude, maintain social connections, and seek fulfillment by prioritizing their personal or professional development and passions. They neither see their lives as liminal nor low status. Bella writes, "When people who are single at heart try to live as part of a couple, they often feel like they are living someone else's life, or like they are wearing a shoe that just does not fit. They are not afraid of being alone; they embrace their solitude, their freedom, and their opportunity to create a life that is uniquely theirs."

If you're fist pumping and shouting "Hallelujah!" you just might be single at heart.

If you skeptically wonder, *"Are* No Ways *really happy alone?"* you are not alone.

For some, to be alone is to be lonely. For example, the US Chamber of Commerce published a list titled "Loneliest Cities in America." Rather than polling people about their levels of loneliness, the Chamber just used the percentage of the adult population living alone as the criterion (Washington, DC, won with 48.2 percent of DC households having one occupant, according to Census Bureau data).

Notable data supports the concerns about loneliness: Compelling scientific evidence reveals how harmful loneliness is psychologically, emotionally, and physically. People's propensity for loneliness is a built-in form of vigilance. For most of human history, being left behind was a death sentence. For hunter-gatherers, belonging to a group was essential for sharing resources and protection. That evolutionary hard wiring and cultural remnants are the underlying contributor to loneliness. The world now allows for greater safety and security, and thus greater discretion for whom you spend time with and for how long. If you are really desperate, you can always attend one of the many loneliness conferences hosted around the world.

There is a huge difference between being alone by choice versus circumstance, as demonstrated by the pain of solitary confinement. The best predictor of loneliness is not being alone, it's wanting to not be alone. Subjective experience matters more than objective experience. Knowing that someone is alone tells you little about whether they are lonely.

Loneliness is a challenge for people who want social or romantic connection and are unable to find it, with young adults and the elderly most at risk. The former is often figuring out how to make adult relationships happen; the latter lack meaningful connections to others (e.g., friends are deceased, kids are absent). While more people are spending more time alone, the real risk is the associated drop in close friendships. Research reveals that not having an answer to the question "Who would you call in the middle of the night when you are sick or afraid?" is associated with poor physical health. My heart aches for the poor souls who can't answer this question—a trend especially dire for men in the United States.

Plenty of *No Ways* have plenty of people to call in the middle of the night. A finding that Bella DePaulo likes to cite is that single people have more friends than married people—a finding replicated in several studies—and it holds true even when single and married people are matched for age, gender, and other factors.

## HERMITS AND HERMETTES

One of my favorite *No Ways* is Risa Mickenberg. The fifty-five-year-old writer, creative director, and performer resides in New York City. Once afraid of being alone, Mickenberg desired marriage and children, later quipping, "I realized that maybe I want to get married just so I can get divorced."

She launched *Hermette Magazine*, a tongue-in-cheek lifestyle magazine for the "recluse by choice" one that "only comes out when it feels like it." Her goal is to glamorize female aloneness. Mickenberg describes a Hermette as the feminization of a hermit—again, tongue firmly in cheek:

> *A Hermette can be any person who's a rugged individualist, an iconoclast, and the steerer of your own ship. It's a person who rejects the typical social constructs, chooses her own life, appreciates time alone and loves being alone, and draws a lot of energy from that. It's an original thinker and a very attractive person. It's somebody who has a force field of protection around them. Your life immediately becomes better when you meet a Hermette.*

Mickenberg relishes when her friends cancel plans, freeing both parties from the obligation to be social. She joked, "I sort of want to tell everybody that I really want to be left the hell alone." Emblematic of their lifestyle, the Hermettes have chosen a fitting mascot. With a shell on its back, the hermit crab has its home with it wherever it goes. A sanctuary tailored for one.

While monks usually live communally as part of a religious community, hermits choose to pursue spiritual growth and contemplation in solitude, often in remote locales.

While this phenomenon is less common now, the hermit as a symbol of spiritual devotion and independence persists in some parts of the world. People historically sought the counsel of hermits during periods of political or social upheaval for spiritual guidance and advice. The hermit lifestyle, defined by self-sufficiency and independence, has been romanticized and admired in many cultures.

It is interesting that eighteenth-century Britain saw a trend of adding hermits to estate grounds. Wealthy landowners constructed hermitages and even offered food, lodging, and a stipend to those willing to live in solitude. Having a resident hermit was seen as a fashionable accessory for the idyllic garden, with visitors often seeking the hermit's spiritual conversation and guidance. Got to keep up with the Joneses!

The term "hermit" is often misunderstood. Hermits spend a lot of time alone, but like other *No Ways*, they are not misanthropes.

Charles Brandt was one such hermit. Brandt was deeply inspired by Henry David Thoreau's *Walden*, a work that celebrated simplicity, self-reliance, and the beauty of nature. It guided him to a remote corner of Vancouver Island. There he lived a life unencumbered by others, embracing the principles of self-reliance and sustainability. He confessed, "I was called to this life."

Brandt was not just any hermit; he was a hermit priest, part of a small group of eight ordained together in 1966. Such was Brandt's dedication to his solitude that he relocated his hermitage miles away from his fellow hermit priests, situating it near the Oyster River at the end of an old logging road, which he called a "road to nowhere."

A thinker, writer, and spiritual soul, Brandt cherished his solitude. Yet he remained tightly woven into the fabric of the Vancouver Island community, leading retreats and meditations for the public. He said: "I am a hermit, and hermits are part of the Church's tradition; we are not isolationists. We are people who have chosen to be alone with the Alone, the great mystery that surrounds us all." His most lasting impression came as a "contemplative activist." An ecologist at heart, he viewed stewardship of the earth as a sacred duty. Through fervent letters and advocacy, he played a pivotal role in community actions that saved rivers from pollution.[1]

Passing away in 2020 at age ninety-seven, he spent fifty-three years as a hermit priest on Vancouver Island. Brandt's legacy persists; his twenty-seven-acre sanctuary is now the Oyster River Hermitage, a public park providing solitude to visitors if they can find it.

The *No Way* lifestyle can be confounding for many people, especially those who are devoted to the escalator, but people like Charles Brandt who choose the *No Way* lifestyle are vital to the larger community because they are often trailblazers and contribute to the world in ways that are difficult for escalator riders. Especially because there are no escalators in the forest.

I wonder how many other remarkable achievements in art, science, entertainment, and advocacy have been made possible by going Solo?

A recent study by Princeton ecologists, published in *Trends in Ecology & Evolution*, suggests both "loner" humans and so-called lone wolves demonstrate crucial roles in collective survival and ecological stability, even helping humanity survive in the case of a mass extinction event. The study highlights how individuals who prefer solitude significantly contribute to ecological diversity, resilience, and disease prevention. Take actual lone wolves as an example: When a wolf leaves its birth pack, becoming a lone wolf—a behavior exhibited by about 15 percent of the species—it plays an indispensable role in population dispersal. These lone wolves traverse great distances to discover new territories and mates, helping to establish new populations, and bridging fragmented populations like "stepping stones." In doing so, they increase essential genetic diversity, contributing to species health and adaptability. Analogously, human "lone wolves," individuals choosing lives of solitude, play vital roles in society, as demonstrated by Brandt's contributions.

For some people, their contribution starts by making a commitment to themselves.

In 1993, in what is suspected to be the first self-marriage ceremony, Linda Barker married in a California chapel, attended by seven bridesmaids and seventy-five guests. Wearing a white dress, she exchanged vows and rings with herself. Her celebration marked a new chapter in her life. Barker's celebration of self-love attracted media attention and put self-marriage on the map and into the minds of thousands of others who have since walked down the aisle alone.*

Also known as "sologamy," self-marriage is increasingly popular among women who seek to simultaneously assert their independence and commitment to themselves. Robbie Fincham, a member of the Solo community, told me about her self-marriage:

> *My self-marriage was a radical act of self-love. This ceremony provided a way for me to publicly commit to loving and honoring myself and celebrate my solo status. It was a profound moment*

---

* If this image seems ridiculous to you, what does it say about the structure of a traditional wedding more generally?

*when I said vows to myself into a full-length mirror, promising to*
*be my own best friend!*

Not surprisingly, a self-marriage wedding-industrial complex
is springing up around the world. For example, the four-day
Marry Oneself Journey at a luxury resort on a private island in
Cozumel goes far beyond the typical "I do." Prices start at $1,300
per night (plus tax) based on single occupancy. This includes
four nights' accommodations, all meals, activities, and the wedding ceremony.

As part of their work on waiting (and non-waiting), Kinneret
Lahad and her coauthor, Michal Kravel-Tovi, turned their attention to self-marriage. They analyzed transcripts of self-marriage
participants talking about their reasons. Expecting to find self-
marriage as a form of Carrie Bradshaw–style resistance against
societal pressures to marry, the researchers were surprised to
discover that many women who practice self-marriage view it as
an act of self-love and commitment to lifelong self-care. A reinvention. Lahad told me, "[It] blew our mind that many of the
women who have articulated or described at length their motivations for self-marriage describe it as an act of self-love, as an
act in which they make a contract with themselves to love themselves." For some women, self-marriage served as a declaration
of "I'm done waiting."

Punk rock taught Rollins the raw energy of forging one's
path, and he, in turn, models how to live on one's own terms.
Let's not forget our front woman, Risa, and her Hermettes who
are free to cancel plans as needed. They are playing the music.
Not just listening to it.

Overlooked by the media, businesses, religious organizations,
and politicians, there's a powerful current running through the

lives of *No Ways*. I resonate deeply with this lifestyle, as I often find myself sailing through *No Way* waters.

What about you, dear reader? Maybe you're not a full-fledged *No Way*, but there's something invigorating about a life without romance. Life can be as vivacious, meaningful, and boundless as you allow it to be. I assure you, society will find *No Ways* impossible to ignore.

## SOLO LOVE LETTER

### Lucy, Host of *Spinster Reimagined* and Women's Coach, London, UK

A few years ago, on a beautiful July evening, I sat on the bench outside my flat and experienced what can only be described as an epiphany. Catching up on some WhatsApp messages with a few of my closest friends about their husbands and children, I noticed that rather than feeling any sense of lack, failure, or being "less than," what I actually felt was a sense of relief. And more than that, it was a feeling of excitement and joy that I myself wasn't married or a mother.

Despite a string of long(ish)-term boyfriends throughout my adult life, what I came to realize—and perhaps accept in that moment— was what I had suspected for some time: that I was (to use Bella DePaulo's term) single at heart. My intuition had been whispering persistently to me for many years, saying, *You're happier on your own.* And the older I get, the more I lean into the fact that I'm just one of those people who is better alone. But more than that, I need to be alone in order to be the best and most actualized version of myself. It's only the ingrained, persistent, and pervasive expectations of the society in which we live that have always led me to believe I should be part of a traditional couple.

But the truth of life is this: We don't find our happiness in any-body else; it has to come from within us. And if we can find the strength to swim against the tide of societal expectation, we will real-ize that—whether or not we end up in a relationship somewhere down the line—our inherent value is to be found in the person looking back at us in the mirror.

Being a Solo isn't always easy—neither is any other life path. But what it absolutely is, is equally deserving of the title "Valid, Valuable, Meaningful Life Path." A Solo life and a coupled life both come with—in equal measure—highs and lows, good bits and bad bits, happiness and sadness, tears and laughter, darkness and light, confusion and clarity, trust and fear, and calm and chaos. Being Solo does not equate to misery and sadness, nor does it equate to loneliness. And by the same token, being married and having chil-dren does not equate to happiness, nor does it equate to a lack of loneliness.

All I can say for sure is that I love my life. And at the age of forty-seven, I'm the happiest I've ever been. I do not feel "less than," I do not feel lack, and I most certainly do not feel like a failure—although that really depends on how you define success. To me, it's about being comfortable and content in my own skin. And that's where I find myself. Life on my own feels more purposeful, powerful, meaningful, and exciting than it ever has in a relationship.

## SOLO LOVE LETTER

### Sarah, Lawyer, London, UK

I thought I was a misfit. I just didn't seem to fit into this couple-shaped world. Coupledom as the only happily-ever-after is the prevailing trope, and I suppose it's natural to want to run with the herd. But it can be life changing to stop running and really think, *Does this actually work for me?*

Whenever I found myself in a relationship, I felt I was shape-shifting into an ill-fitting space. I'd end up pining for me-time and become keenly aware of the opportunity cost of the relationship. I'd get through the hell of the apps only to arrive at a status that didn't much suit me anyway.

When the pandemic came along and it became practically against the law to date, I was set free! State-sanctioned orders to stay home, grow out your roots, and rock hairy legs in pj's. Coupledom was off the table, and I felt a huge sense of relief. Time to stop lady gardening and start real gardening!

I moved into me. I learned to be by myself. I gave up drinking—a complete change. I started exercising, I changed my job, and I never colored my hair again.

I'm more at ease and content in myself today than I have ever really been. Not dating has freed up time for many more people in my life—as they say, it takes a village. I am so grateful for the freedom and independence I enjoy. And I know now that I'm not a misfit in this world after all. I'm quite the opposite, I'm part of a new wave.

I'm a *Proud Single*. As I tell my friends who want me to partner up, "I'm a *Pringle!*"

# EIGHT

## New Way

As a podcaster and speaker who unapologetically celebrates singlehood and supports the pursuit of unconventional relationships, people open up to me in unexpected ways:

- A stand-up comedian told me that he only dates single moms. He wants to be the third most important thing in her life, after her kids and job.
- A thirty-something, Washington, DC, policy wonk described how she likes to date couples. The couple she was dating at that time would see her together or individually.
- A pregnant, polyamorous mother-of-one announced that she was seeking casual, consensual sex with no strings attached.

So, I was not surprised when I met Josh Gray-Emmer at a Downtown Los Angeles (DTLA) coffee shop, and he nonchalantly mentioned, "I date my friends and sleep with strangers."

DTLA Josh, as I call him, is deeply committed to friendship. He hosts the DTLA Dinner Club, a weekly event where thirty people gather at his home for a free celebrity-chef-prepared dinner. The meal provides an opportunity for new acquaintances to get to know his friends. The consummate host, he also brings friends together weekly for "Dim Sum Sundays" and "Bro Drink Fridays." ("Bro" is a state of mind, as women are welcome to attend the after-hours party.)

The forty-five-year-old's love life, on the other hand, is comprised of strangers. Literally. His staccato description of his method is as follows: "I will turn on my phone. I will turn on Grindr. It will start beeping. I will pick out who I want. They will show up. We will hook up. They will leave." Josh does not mince his words, nor mix his worlds. The strangers he sleeps with are not invited to dim sum.

DTLA Josh is a *New Way* Solo. Unapologetically so.

*No Ways* are single by choice. Some *Just Mays* and *Somedays* are single by chance; they may not currently have a partner, but they seek a fellow escalator rider.

There is an overlooked group—singles by mismatch—that took me years to recognize, perhaps because I was a member. The person is fortunate enough to find dates but struggles to find a good match because their dates only want to ride the escalator (most people want that, after all). If singles by mismatch do partner up, moreover, the person struggles in a relationship because of the friction caused by differing desires. These singles by mismatch strive and struggle, often concluding that there is something wrong with them for not being able to make the relationship escalator "work."

We're told that an escalator relationship is the ideal state of being. This assumption often leads people to devalue other important connections, such as friendships or familial relationships, and can pressure people to pursue and prioritize one style of romantic relationship above all else.

Family, friends, and therapists often don't help, urging these singles by mismatch to be "better" at riding the escalator. Put aside childish ways. Get serious. Try harder!

One of these singles is Frank, a smart, insightful comedian who occasionally has a girlfriend. Frank lives a remarkable life, but at some point, his girlfriend becomes unhappy that things are not moving along "the way they ought to." Frank is "too into his career." He is "not attentive enough." None of these statements are untrue. Frank is "married to comedy."

The couple will end up in therapy where his girlfriend and the therapist team up to harangue him for not wanting "it" enough. Put aside childish ways. Get serious. Try harder!

I know the feeling.

Why can't Frank make a relationship work with these wonderful women? Most singles by mismatch assume that there is something wrong with them. Frank is the first to acknowledge his deficiencies—he jokes about them onstage. However, that is not the problem. Though he likes to date and welcomes romance, he has other priorities that get in the way of a full ride on the relationship escalator. Trying to date the wrong type of person, we independently shared the epiphany: "I'm not broken. The escalator is."

Frank is not alone. A lot of people want something different. Maybe slightly different. Maybe strikingly different.

They:
- want a friends with benefits (FWB) situation
- want mostly friends, a few with benefits
- want their partner to be a neighbor, not a roommate
- want multiple romantic or sexual partners
- want a platonic partnership

- want tenderness, affection, and companionship, but not sex (e.g., a cuddle buddy)
- desire a once-a-week date night with no communication in between
- have no interest in sex or romance or both
- want a co-parent but not a romantic partner
- frequent sex clubs with a partner, partners, or alone

Or any other unconventional relationship within the bounds of the law.

These are the *New Way* Solos, people who desire relationships, perhaps romantic and/or intimate, but not necessarily adhering to the relationship escalator model.

The *New Way* solution is not to work harder to fit the escalator model, but rather to seek out unconventional relationships that align with their unique desires. They bend or break the rules of the escalator to create relationships that fit for them.

Let's briefly revisit the rules of the escalator:

**Hierarchy:** The relationship should be the most important adult–adult relationship in one's life. The other person often has wide-ranging "veto" power.

**Merging:** Escalator riders should join their lives by way of living arrangement, finances, and even identity.

**Consistent sexual and romantic monogamy:** An exclusive relationship that starts and doesn't stop. People in the relationship are not allowed to be intimate or romantic with others.

Amatonormativity, the societal expectation that everyone is or should be following the rules of the escalator, is evidenced by the typical dating app, filled with singles who want that traditional progression through milestones of increasing attachment: dating, moving in, marrying, and starting a family. They are quick to reject and perhaps demean people who want a relationship that relaxes or removes the escalator's rules:

- "No hookups. No FWBs."
- "Swipe left if you are into ENM!"
- "Polyamorous? Not here."*

Sometimes, I am a *No Way*, and sometimes I am a proud *New Way*. It's been exciting to learn about the vast array of alternative lifestyles people are pursuing. I've got ninety-nine problems but the escalator ain't one.

## IF NOT THE ESCALATOR?

As a reminder to singles by mismatch being shamed by family, friends, and strangers on the apps, the escalator rules are *made up*. The rules have not always existed and are not necessarily inherent to human nature. Although a deeply ingrained part of our current domestication, these rules can be adjusted.

I have chosen solitude over shared space, living alone for all of my adulthood except for a four-year hiatus in college and grad school. My own step off the relationship escalator started with my dedication to living alone, which was the cause of two major breakups in my life. Moving in with someone—no matter how wonderful the person or the relationship—is a nonstarter for me. Once a source of heartache when my partner discovered this too late, I now politely disclose my preference early on when

---

* To illustrate the moral superiority associated with the escalator, imagine the reactions if someone on the dating apps were to put in their bio, "Swipe left if you are into monogomy!" or "Looking for marriage? Not here."

I have a new love interest. My dates appreciate the honesty. I have had women "high-five" me across the table and others engage in thoughtful, curious conversation about my desires, and others bring the date to a quick conclusion "Check, please!"

Learning that people are increasingly rejecting amatonormativity gives me hope that I *may* find someone to date who would welcome that life choice, and encourages me to challenge other societal norms that no longer serve me.

My path to the *New Way* philosophy was informed by a friend whom I witnessed stumble his way to Solohood. When I met Fernando ten-plus years ago, he had recently moved on from "sport fucking," as he called it, to attempt a life as a *Someday* single.

Fernando can ride the escalator—to a point. He joked, "I may be the horse you ride, but not the one you bet on." A serial monogamist, his pattern included moving in with a girlfriend for a few years before he would start to feel trapped and be tempted to cheat.

Fernando was so frustrated that he couldn't make the escalator work that he eventually gave up and went full lone wolf. "Doomed to be a loner," he tried the *No Way* life, but missed emotional, physical, and sensual connections. A revelation occurred when he discovered a world of alternatives on a dating app that serves the *New Way* crowd. Fernando's desire was to find a primary romantic partner, while engaging in occasional sexual play and exploration.

Dan Savage, syndicated sex advice columnist and ever the provocateur, calls Fernando's preference "monogamish."

Fernando calls himself "90 percent monogamous."

He moved to Berlin (perhaps the *New Way* capital of the world), and as he settled into this new lifestyle, he met a woman who shared his perspective. While discussing their proclivities for deep emotional connections and playful dalliances, she remarked, "Why not have it all?" They began to date, moved in together, and would go to the occasional sex party or invite a guest star into the bedroom.

Fernando sums up his progression as "thesis" (*Someday*) to "antithesis" (*No Way*) to "synthesis" (*New Way*).

## Nonmonogamy, A Case Study

In the 2005 documentary *March of the Penguins*, emperor penguins are shown as monogamous during breeding season. Religious leaders were enthralled by these images and started referencing the movie in sermons and newsletters, urging their followers to be inspired by the penguins' devotion. Religious organizations even began hosting free movie nights, featuring the film with follow-up discussions to promote a message to remain faithful.

The truth is, while emperor penguins display impressive devotion to each other during the breeding season, they do not remain together. These penguins often find new mates each breeding season and spend very little time together during the rest of the year. Even the monogamous southern rockhopper penguins, who supposedly mate for life, only spend about twenty to thirty days a year together. Actually, this sounds like a lot of successful marriages.

Nonmonogamy is overwhelmingly the norm in the animal kingdom. A more accurate documentary could instead be set in a forest in the Democratic Republic of the Congo featuring bonobos, an endangered great ape. These evolutionary cousins of ours use sex as a social tool for bartering, forming alliances, and resolving conflicts. Anthropologists, sociologists, and historians who have studied nonmonogamy assert that nonmonogamy has been prevalent throughout human history. Joseph Henrich contends that 85 percent of societies have had polygamous marriages at some point.

The most important rule of the escalator is that the relationship is "closed" by way of consistent romantic and sexual monogamy. The rule is also the most frequently broken, either by way of cheating (nonconsensual nonmonogamy) or by consensual nonmonogamy. Finally, the rule is the most "moral" of the rules, and thus to many, nonmonogamous behavior is seen as not just wrong, but immoral. Nevertheless, when nonmonogamy is executed without harm (i.e., consensually) it ceases to hold moral sway.

A YouGov poll from January 2020 reveals increasing interest and more positive attitudes toward consensual nonmonogamy, with 32 percent of US adults considering their ideal relationship to be nonmonogamous to some degree. Consensual nonmonogamy (or ethical nonmonogamy) occurs when parties agree on and acknowledge the presence of multiple romantic and/or sexual relationships. The practice is distinct from nonconsensual nonmonogamy (aka cheating).

You may recall that monogamy is not about what escalator riders can do, but rather what riders cannot do. Participants are not allowed to share sexual or romantic intimacy with anyone outside of the primary relationship, despite a lack of guarantees that they will continue to have sex or romance with each other. Exclusivity applies even if sex or romance wanes. Along those lines, I have a friend whose mom decided that she didn't want to have sex with her husband anymore. Fair enough, but when I asked if her dad could take a lover or hire a sex worker to fulfill his needs, my friend looked at me as if I were a degenerate.

Whether monogamous or nonmonogamous, people often wrestle with jealousy. The consensual nonmonogamy community, in turn, promotes the idea of "compersion," or anti-jealousy, which refers to the positive feelings experienced when a partner has positive experiences with other people. This is a tricky one for most people who would be happy that their partner has a fun night out with friends, but would struggle being happy that their partner has a fun night out on a date. Yet, some people can be happy with both situations.

## RELAXING OR REMOVING RULES

Unconventional relationships change the rules of the escalator—sometimes radically. In figure 5, I present a non-exhaustive list of unconventional romantic, sexual, and platonic relationships. The figure shows definitions, and the rules of the escalator that participants either adhere to, discard, or make optional, depending on the relationship and those in it.

In the top row of the figure is the escalator, where all the rules are present. In the bottom row is relationship design, where all the escalator rules (and more) are up for negotiation. I will cover relationship design in the next chapter.

Let's look at the unconventional relationships in the figure, in turn.

### Solo Monogamy

Solo monogamists ride the escalator and follow all its rules with the exception of merging their living arrangement, finances, and/or lifestyle. Solo monogamy goes by various names, including "Apartners," "Living Apart Together," "Dual-Dwelling Duos," and "Committed Non-Cohabitation."

| | | Merging | Hierarchy | Consistency | Sexual Exclusivity | Romantic Exclusivity |
|---|---|---|---|---|---|---|
| **Relationship Type** | **Definition** | | | | | |
| Relationship Escalator | A traditional monogamous progression through visible milestones of increasing attachment including dating, cohabitating, marrying, and starting a family. | Yes | Yes | Yes | Yes | Yes |
| Solo Monogamy | Embracing monogamy while valuing personal autonomy and independence, without seeking to merge lives with a significant other. | No | Yes | Yes | Yes | Yes |
| Swinging | A lifestyle of nonmonogamy where non-committal, rule-limited sexual activities occur outside of the established couple, often involving partner swapping. | Yes | Yes | Yes | No | Yes |
| Polyamory | Maintaining multiple, consensual, and loving connections with various partners at the same time. | Maybe | Maybe | Yes | No | No |
| Solo Polyamory | Prioritizing personal autonomy in a nonmonogamous lifestyle without seeking to merge lives with partners. | No | Maybe | Yes | No | No |
| Friends | A connection based on mutual affection, trust, and support that does not involve romance or physical intimacy. | No | Maybe | Maybe | No | No |
| Friends with Benefits/Sexual Relationships | A casual, non-romantic friendship that includes physical intimacy, without commitment or an expectation of exclusivity. | No | Maybe | Maybe | No | No |
| Platonic Partnership | A close, emotionally intimate bond without romantic attachment, often involving shared living arrangements and life goals (aka "Chosen Family"). | Yes | Yes | Yes | No | No |
| Relationship Design | An intentional act of cocreating a customized relationship, in which all parties agree on the rules and regularly revisit the agreement, revising as necessary. | Maybe | Maybe | Maybe | Maybe | Maybe |

**FIGURE 5:** Common unconventional relationship types, their definitions, and how they adhere or diverge from rules of the relationship escalator.

According to the US Census Bureau's American Community Survey, 1.7 million married couples, or 3 percent of the total population, are taking "I need some space" to a whole new level. Even when people live together, they may not share the same bed. A 2017 survey by the Better Sleep Council discovered that a surprising 26 percent of couples were snoozing separately.

Cue the onslaught of articles, advice columns, and raised eyebrows from escalator riders who can't quite wrap their head around an Apartnership. A friend's mother, for example, is vocal that my friend should share the same *blanket* as her spouse. I ask if they are supposed to share the same toothbrush?

## Swinging

Swinging involves couples being semi-committed to sexual monogamy. While remaining predominantly on the escalator, swingers usually partake in regulated, no-strings-attached, sexual encounters with other couples or individuals. They might exchange partners or include a "guest star" or "unicorn" in their tryst. Motivations for swinging vary greatly: to explore sexual desires and fantasies, seek sexual experimentation and variety, or find a community of like-minded people.

Swinging is the most common unconventional relationship, but doesn't align comfortably with either escalator riders or other members of the "lifestyle" community. On one hand, swingers don't fit with the traditional escalator crowd who often view them as too threatening to invite to dinner parties. Will our swinging guests try to seduce someone into the swinging life-style, even pilfer a partner? On the other hand, those who have more aggressively stepped off the relationship escalator judge swingers for being committed to the merging and hierarchy norms of the escalator. Opinions. Everyone seems to have one.

## Polyamory and Solo Polyamory

Polyamory is derived from the Greek word "poly," meaning "many," and the Latin word "amor," meaning "love," and refers to the practice of maintaining multiple, consensual, loving connections with various partners at the same time. The term was coined by Morning Glory Zell-Ravenheart in 1990, and awareness of the relationship style has blossomed in recent years.

"Poly" is suddenly all over the dating apps, with people expressing their desire or aversion.

Polyamory has different forms, with varying levels of interconnectedness between participants. A polyamory "vee" exists where one person dates multiple people who do not have a romantic connection with one another. Triads, quads, and other closed relationships typically limit sexual and romantic relationships to an established group.

Solo polyamory prioritizes personal autonomy in a nonmonogamous lifestyle. Solo polyamorists don't want to merge their life with any of their partners and emphasize individual independence and sovereignty within a nonmonogamous context. Solo polyamorous practitioners often eschew the typical relationship hierarchy in which one partner is considered a "primary," while others hold a "secondary" or "tertiary" status. Instead, Solo poly folks are focused on forging connections that prioritize respect of each partner's autonomy.

Polyamory of any variety presents unique challenges, such as managing time, emotional labor, and communication among multiple partners. Relationships take work, and in this case, there are more relationships that require nurturing. Laura Grant, a proud Solo, friend, and Solo polyamorist, says: "Rejecting the scarcity model of love can be expansive and rewarding; but although love is infinite, time and personal bandwidth are not. When a new world of opportunities presents itself, it takes discipline and self-awareness to know your own limits, and to mindfully invest in each relationship instead of spreading oneself too thin." Despite these challenges, Elisabeth Sheff, in her book *The Polyamorists Next Door: Inside Multiple-Partner Relationships and Families*, documents how people in polyamorous relationships report high levels of satisfaction, trust, and communication, and lower levels of jealousy compared to monogamous people.

### Friends (with Benefits)

I am obsessed with friendship—bonds based on mutual affection, trust, and support, but devoid of romance or physical intimacy. One remarkable aspect of friendships is the ability to bend the rules of continuity. Friends may go days, weeks, months, or even years without contact, for example, yet when they come together, it is as if nothing has changed.

I tell my friends I love them. The notion of platonic love, developed in Plato's *Symposium*, once focused on wisdom and truth, and over time has evolved to include deep, non-romantic and nonsexual friendships. Now, platonic love emphasizes emotional and intellectual connection rather than romantic or sexual feelings.

In her book *Love 2.0: How Our Supreme Emotion Affects Everything We Feel, Think, Do, and Become,* psychologist Barbara Fredrickson defines love as "micro-moments of positivity resonance." That is a rather nerdy way to say that most loving moments are a fleeting experience that arise when people share positive emotions and a sense of mutual care. Thus, most love in the world is not the long-lasting, swoony connection of a soulmate. People can have loving moments with family, friends, and even strangers.

Although friendship by definition is devoid of physical intimacy, friends with benefits (FWB), or "sexual friendships," challenge this belief. These are friendships that involve sexual intimacy—monogamous or not—but rarely romance. Research suggests that friends-with-benefits relationships are relatively common, particularly among young adults. A 2014 study published in the journal *Archives of Sexual Behavior* found that roughly 60 percent of college students have had an FWB.

Friends with benefits manifest in various forms besides the obvious. Consider the "comet" relationship. A term popularized by sex advice columnist Dan Savage, this phenomenon involves intermittent yet intense connections. Jessalyn Dean is a friend and an aromantic individual who dates and simultaneously maintains several intimate and platonic relationships. She told me about her comet, a sexual partner in Germany with whom she only meets when they are in the same city. They may go two-plus years without connecting, but when they do, it is as if nothing has changed.

## Platonic Partnership

Amatonormativity ingrains the notion that romantic relationships should always take precedence over friendships. Not everyone subscribes to this hierarchy. Platonic partnerships lack sexual and romantic connections, but they are no less meaningful to the participants. Elevating friendship is an act of rebellion against romantic veto power.

I spoke to Rhaina Cohen about a story that appears in her book, *The Other Significant Others: Reimagining Life with Friendship at the Center.* Cohen tells the story of Kami and Tilly, who prioritize their deep friendship over romantic relationships. They still date, but the platonic relationship comes first. In the story, Kami meets a man whom she starts dating, and tells him early on: "Just so you know, she's always going to come first. It's not going to change."

Cohen later told me what happened. "The first guy Kami made that comment to didn't last long but she did give the same spiel to her current partner, who she's been with for quite a while and has a child with."

Two women living together in a close, platonic relationship in Boston in the late 1800s and early 1900s was called a Boston marriage. Some of the couplings were romantic, but for many it provided a way for women to support each other while challenging traditional gender roles. Today, Boston marriage is used more broadly to describe close friendships between women, such as Aminatou Sow and Ann Friedman—best friends who use the term "big friendship" to describe the strength and depth of their bond. A noteworthy example is the profound platonic love between Iris Murdoch and Philippa Foot, two prominent British philosophers and brilliant minds who met at Oxford University in the early 1940s. While their relationship started as a brief romantic one, it eventually evolved into a lifelong intellectual and emotional bond free of sex and romance.

A major concern for platonic partners is that they don't receive the benefits or legal protections of a romantic marriage. That is why a recent Swedish Supreme Court decision was so groundbreaking when it ruled in favor of a surviving platonic partner in a case that centered on the legitimacy of their nonsexual relationship. This ruling set a significant precedent, recognizing that relationships should not be measured solely by sexual or romantic metrics. By acknowledging that platonic relationships can be significant, this decision challenges conventional views on what constitutes a meaningful relationship.

## Asexuality and Aromanticism

Riding the escalator is challenging when someone desires an emotional connection but is disinterested in sex, or when someone desires sexual intimacy but is disinterested in romance. At least 1 percent of the population identifies with these sentiments.

Asexuality is an orientation where a person does not experience sexual attraction toward others. Asexuality exists on a spectrum, where some people are repulsed by sexual activity, others simply lack desire, and some may still engage in sexual activities despite their lack of sexual attraction. Asexuality is a natural part of a person's identity, just like being heterosexual, homosexual, or bisexual. Asexuality is different from celibacy, which is a choice to abstain from sex when a motivation is present.

Aromanticism is an orientation where a person does not experience romantic attraction toward others. Aromantic people may not have the desire to engage in romantic relationships, but can still form strong emotional bonds and friendships. Like asexuality, aromanticism also exists on a spectrum, with some people experiencing little or no romantic attraction, while others may experience it occasionally or under specific circumstances.

I had a conversation with David Jay, a prominent activist behind Asexuality.org and the Asexual Visibility and Education Network. He has been instrumental in raising awareness about asexuality and contributed to the delisting of asexuality as a mental disorder from the *Diagnostic and Statistical Manual of Mental Disorders* (*DSM*) in 2013.

Aromanticism and asexuality can be experienced independently: romantic asexual, aromantic sexual, or aromantic asexual. Jay told me:

*I still have a desire to form close emotional relationships, just not to make sexuality a part of them. But there's a bunch of different ways that asexuality shows up. Some people still have a strong romantic attraction. They might identify as homoromantic or heteroromantic. They might still date people. They might still want a romantic, long-term partnership. I, along with a lot of asexual people, identify as aromantic. I tend to form close committed friendships—I would call them aromantic partnerships—rather than romantic relationships.*

Jay wanted to have kids and took a *New Way* approach to satisfy that desire. He is the father of two children born through in vitro fertilization whom he is co-raising with aromantic partners.

## NEW WAYS OF MARRIAGE AND PARENTING

The invention of Coke led to the invention of Diet Coke, Cherry Coke, Vanilla Coke, and Coke Zero. The same is true for the invention of marriage. In her book *Sex and Temperament in Three Primitive Societies*, Margaret Mead examined alternative forms of societal expectations of men, women, and their children in these societies. The Mundugumor people of Papua New Guinea practiced "pairing marriage," in which couples live together for a period of time before deciding whether to get married. The Arapesh people of Papua New Guinea instead practiced "community marriages," where groups of men and women engage in sexual relationships with one another without exclusive pairings or long-term commitments. The Tchambuli people of Papua New Guinea instead practice "complementary marriage," in which the roles of men and women were reversed compared to contemporary society.

In their book, *The New I Do: Reshaping Marriage for Skeptics, Realists, and Rebels*, Vicki Larson and Susan Pease Gadoua cover an array of alternative forms of marriage. For example, a "trial run" marriage features a time-limited, child-free marital arrangement that allows couples to explore the experience of commitment without the expectation of permanence. A "security-oriented" marriage may be chosen with the goal of providing emotional and financial stability, whereas a "sacred pact" marriage is a more traditional, religion-rooted marriage that emphasizes the importance of faith and commitment.

Parenthood is a goal for many singles and non-singles alike. According to the latest data from the US Census Bureau, 85 percent of women and 79 percent of men in the United States become parents by age forty-five—though those rates are dropping. Another *New Way* approach is for people to unite for the main purpose of having children—to co-parent rather than follow the traditional relationship escalator.

Some people are doing away with a co-parent altogether. These solo parents take on the challenge of raising children on their own. In some cases, this is due to the other parent being unable to or unwilling to participate in parenting. In other cases, it is a choice. For example, Mindy Kaling, the actor, comedian, writer, and producer best known for *The Office* and *The Mindy Project*, became a single mother by choice at age thirty-eight and again at forty-one.

It is one thing to choose to go it alone as a parent with Hollywood money, but it's more challenging with middle-class means. *Solo* podcast guests Paula Wood and Marla Cichowski are two mothers who came to be single parents in different ways. Paula had an "oopsie" pregnancy and decided to parent alone, while Marla sought out a sperm donor. Marla told us:

> *When I was twenty-five, I thought,* If I'm not married by the time I'm thirty with probably at least one kid on the way by the time I'm thirty-two, then the world may stop rotating. *I couldn't imagine what my life would look like if those things had not happened at that age. At forty, I had gotten out of a relationship not too long before that and I was like, "Here we go. Where are*

*we going? What am I doing?" I know so many women who have*
*walked in those footsteps. I know being a parent is not for everyone.*
*I have always felt in my heart that somehow, someway, I would*
*become a mother.*

They told me stories of how rewarding the experiences were,
but were honest about the nontrivial time, energy, and financial commitments that accompany the other challenges of parenthood. Moreover, they faced snide comments and stereotypes
from society, whether on a date or interacting with a sales asso-
ciate. A common comfort was found in communities of friends,
family, and other Solo parents to whom they could go for
support.

## Role models

The *New Ways* herein invite you to question how well conventional norms fit your desires and aspirations. They encourage
you to bend the rules, break them, or redefine them to find
fulfillment in romantic, sexual, non-romantic, or nonsexual
connections. Ultimately, these perspectives may inspire you to
challenge the domestication that creates divisions and leaves
people feeling excluded.

I could fill an entire book about *New Ways* and their unconventional relationships. This chapter was designed to stir your curiosity, challenge your preconceptions, or validate your existing
unconventional choices. If you're seeking a deeper understanding of unconventional relationship structures, I recommend
starting with *The Ethical Slut* by Dossie Easton and Janet Hardy or
*Stepping Off the Relationship Escalator* by Amy Gahran.

For some readers, these ideas might be new, radical, even
"gross." I encourage you to keep an open mind, observe how
these concepts play out in other people's lives, and reflect on

how little they impact your life. There's no obligation to dive into a polyamorous relationship if it doesn't align with your preferences. Still, there's immense value in possessing a willingness to choose the kinds of relationships that enhance your life.

## SOLO LOVE LETTER

### Laura, Spreadsheet Artist, Denver, Colorado, USA

While in the process of regrouping after another big breakup in my mid-thirties, I reflected on my dating history, and what was working and bringing me joy and fulfillment. Looking at it through a more constructive lens (and putting my data analysis skills to work on this problem), I realized that my favorite part of dating was when I was searching for a new partner. I was putting myself out there, connecting with and meeting lots of new people, and being curious about what might develop with each unique person I met.

I falsely concluded that I could thus only "play the field" and never move beyond the flirtatious phase of dating around. I would live in that space perpetually, I told myself, and never move on to the next step of "down-selecting to Mr. Right." This seemed like an acceptable plan . . . until I fell in love again.

After a few months of dating, my partner expressed his interest in taking our blossoming romance to the next stage (on the relationship escalator), which for both of us had always included romantic and sexual monogamy. I knew this wasn't a part of my newfound "Playing the Field in Perpetuity" game plan, but I was also very fond of him and wanted to give this relationship as much of a shot as possible. I laid my cards on the table: I wanted our relationship to grow and deepen, but not at the expense of my autonomy and ability to connect with others (sexually, romantically, or otherwise). I was dedicated to being a committed, loving, supportive partner to him . . . just without the exclusivity.

To my shock and delight, he was willing to give that a try.

A door opened that day, leading me down a whole new path. Through a healthy dose of trial and error, and eventually the discovery of polyamory and the language and ethics surrounding it, I had found a model that allowed me to blossom and thrive. I now identify as a solo polyamorist, and place my relationship with myself as of utmost importance. I cherish all my loving partnerships, friends with benefits, and platonic friendships, and connect with new people organically as the opportunities arise. Discovering new language, researching and practicing these concepts, and meeting others who were living this way were pivotal steps toward living more authentically as myself.

## SOLO LOVE LETTER

**Laura, Environmental Educator, Grand Cayman, Cayman Islands**

To me, living Solo means feeling confident in the possibility of living my life independently.

A few years ago, I realized I was asexual and accepted that I didn't need to be following anyone's relationship timelines or structures. Finally, there was another factor in not feeling the want for a partner. Having a language to explain what I was feeling and finding groups of like-minded people (thanks, internet!) helped me feel more confident in living outside the norm. I now know that I can live a fulfilling and happy life Solo, investing my time in hobbies, friendships, and myself.

I may change my mind, but right now I'm not looking for romantic relationships. I don't want the stress and obligation of a partner, nor do I want to share my living space. I don't want a family or kids, and I don't feel like I'm lacking.

I absolutely love that I can make a career change, move to a new place, or travel for months at a time without consulting anyone else. I've got long-distance friends, and I have the time and energy to keep in touch with them. I have the space to work on my mental health, start new hobbies (have y'all tried free diving?), and bake to my heart's content. The journey to feeling like "This is okay and I'm normal to want these things" has been a long one but I'm so glad I'm here.

Even now, while I feel really confident in my decision to live independently, people question this choice. "You moved here alone?" "You don't have a partner?" "You don't want kids?" And that's okay. Every time I reassess my life and decisions, I come to the same conclusion: There are so many different ways to enjoy life, and I'm not hurting anyone by being Solo and happy.

# NINE

# Relationship Design

R obert Frost famously wrote, "Two roads diverged in a yellow wood . . . and I— / I took the one less traveled by, / And that has made all the difference."

*New Ways* have more than two choices, but what if instead of two, twenty, or even two hundred roads to choose from, there was an infinite number?

Welcome to relationship design.

*New Way* Solos are removing or relaxing the escalator's rules to create new ways of relating—romantic or otherwise. However, if you can bend or break a few rules to improve your relationship match, why can't you examine and negotiate *all* the rules?

Changes can be small or big. You don't have to start swinging to use the principles of relationship design. A relationship design agreement could be about veto power. Or sleeping in separate bedrooms. Or coordinating different bedtimes. Or whether you want a good night text.

I was introduced to these ideas by Andie Nordgren, a Swedish game designer, producer, and advocate. Nordgren wrote "The Short Instructional Manifesto for Relationship Anarchy," a 2006 essay that presents a process for defining relationships to suit the participants' needs and desires, rather than defaulting into the rules expected by society. The essay sparked a movement that teaches people how to customize relationships by prioritizing their own desires over societal expectations.

The title introduced Relationship Anarchy, which was originally named Radical Relationships. Unfortunately, the connotations of "anarchy" are often negative and associated with chaos or violence. Some people who understand its literal meaning still mistakenly believe it advocates for relationships without any governing rules.* Nordgren's essay is profoundly useful and has inspired other resources, including Mark A. Michaels and Patricia Johnson's book, *Designer Relationships: A Guide to Happy Monogamy, Positive Polyamory, and Optimistic Open Relationships,* which further expanded these ideas.

I will present an amalgamation of these perspectives here, with a Solo touch.

**Relationship design is the process by which two or more people intentionally engage in cocreating a customized relationship, in which all parties agree on the rules and regularly revisit the agreement, revising as necessary.**

The benefits of relationship design are profound. Besides creating better connections, designers improve their communication skills, embrace vulnerability, and foster greater trust. Learning how to let go of default norms and negotiate personalized connections enables the creation of a customized

---

* The earliest recorded use of "anarchy" meant an "absence of government." The term was later used to reference a utopian society that had no government. It further can be used to mean a state of confusion or disorder. More broadly, anarchy is "not ruled by a group, tyrant, hierarchy, authority, or other centralized rule making and enforcing body." Which means that anarchy can include rules, though they are enforced through self-governance or through the effective group in its entirety. Unfortunately, misconceptions about the name make relationship anarchy a less-than-appealing moniker for something quite appealing.

relationship that can be more honest, open-hearted, and effective. While no relationship is perfect, I contend that this approach allows for the creation of relationships that are ideally suited to the unique combination of tastes, wants, and desires of the people involved.

In this chapter, I focus on romance, sex, and friendships. However, it's important to note that relationship design principles can be applied to a wide array of interpersonal bonds, both conventional and unconventional, including those among siblings, coworkers, and even between parents and kids.

## ASK FOR WHAT YOU WANT

When my friend Jessalyn Dean matches with someone on a dating app, the other party eventually asks what she "wants." She somewhat robotically answers, "I'm looking for the Venn diagram where your wants and needs overlap my wants and needs." In that spirit, she practices her own version of relationship design. She likens her approach to selecting tapas to share with others. Imagine a huge table with a variety of different plates, like if Cheesecake Factory did tapas. The people at the table look at the tapas and agree on the ones that they want to share, ignoring all the others. There may be some negotiating over which tapas to choose, but everyone feels satisfied. Of course, different people at the table would choose a meal comprising different tapas.

If it isn't obvious from the analogy, each tapa is an agreement for the relationship. One tapa may be "I want to spend the night after sex," or conversely, "I want to sleep alone." Another tapa might be about how to obtain a partner's consent before a non-monogamous dalliance, and another might be about how often they see each other in a week.

It is important for relationship designers to recognize and voice their opinions on the default rules or social norms governing conventional relationships, whether these are micro or macro in nature. For example, merging is a macro rule where escalator riders will become intertwined: living arrangement, finances, and/or lifestyle. Micro rules may be more likely to be implicit, but often should be articulated. A micro rule for heterosexual couples (which may change because of merging finances, for example) might be that the man may not be solely responsible for paying for dates.

Relationships typically require communication regarding the rules and expectations that are present, but it becomes critical when departing from standard scripts. Macro assumptions, for example, may include statements such as:

"I want to live with a partner, but I am in no rush."

"I would consider living with someone, but it depends on the person."

"I am not comfortable with sharing a bank account, but I am willing to discuss shared expenses."

"I want to maintain my career. I won't move to a new city for any relationship."

"I would like our relationship to allow for separate vacations."

"I would marry, but only for practical reasons such as tax benefits or health insurance."

You can imagine the variety of questions and answers that could further delineate and clarify these preferences. Working toward an agreement, simple answers such as "Yes," "No," or "Maybe" can be useful. Another approach categorizes preferences as "Flexible," "Must have," "Nice to have," or "Deal breaker."

Discussing overarching macro agreements may lead to evaluations of micro agreements. For example, a perspective on merging might be: "I want to merge our finances, but I would like to keep my existing retirement account separate. Any money invested moving forward would be for both of us together." Or "I would like the temperature in the bedroom to be sixty-eight degrees or lower in the winter." A micro agreement unrelated to merging could be something like, "I would like to have a once-a-week date night, no matter how busy we get—even if we have a child." Or, "Rather than texting, I want to talk on the phone when doing in-depth planning."

Many of the above examples are instances of "design by inclusion," discussing the desired elements in a relationship. However, it's important to acknowledge "design by exclusion" as a valid and potent approach to relationship design. For example:

- "I don't want to live with my partner."
- "I do not want children, but I am okay if you already have children from previous relationships."
- "I am uncomfortable with public displays of affection."

Ultimately, through open communication and negotiation, relationship design empowers people to craft relationships that are deeply aligned with their values and needs.

## Prototype. Evaluate. Iterate.

Relationship design is inspired by design principles, which typically involve problem-solving, empathy, collaboration, prototyping, evaluating, and iterative testing.

Professional designers will often prototype a solution or product, which means they create a preliminary model or version to test and improve upon. In relationship design, the agreements are discussed and set to form an early version of a "container" that metaphorically holds the relationship. I like

the container metaphor because its form represents the agreements, expectations, and boundaries that encompass the
relationship.

The relationship escalator is a premade container with clear
expectations. Eli Finkel, the author of the *All-or-Nothing Marriage*,
told me the story of an imaginary couple. Jasmine, as a single
twenty-eight-year-old, has a diverse social network. For instance,
she attends yoga classes with her friend Kyoko and studies for
the MCAT with her friend John. You can imagine how the list
goes on. A friend to have coffee with. A friend who likes hiking.
A friend whose shoulder she can cry on. Jasmine has love in her
heart for these people.

Finkel highlights how this scenario shifts when Jasmine is
married at forty. Now, she relies on her spouse to fulfill most of
her needs. Perhaps her husband is great at meeting all these
needs, from being a yoga partner to offering emotional support. But what if he is not? Maybe he rolls his eyes at the
metaphysical aspects of yoga, but he will go hiking anytime his
baby wants! Finkel told me, "I push hard for people to be specific." Finkel explains, "What is it that we're going to look
for from each other? What is it that we're demanding of the
marriage?"

Relationship design would reveal where Jasmine and her
spouse should be spending their time together and where they
should rely on other relationships for support and fulfillment.
They would discover where they can coordinate and when they
need to compromise. The couple would not default into the
social norms of "all or nothing."

Coordination rather than compromise is preferred when creating a relationship container. What often happens with a "pre-
packaged relationship" is that even if the macro agreement is a
fit, one or more of the participants will find some element less

than desirable. Two becoming one may require substantial compromise. Couples must navigate differences in preferences and habits in the bedroom, bathroom, and beyond. Compatibility with bed times, room temperatures, vacation destinations, hobbies, social lives, and family visits make a relationship more likely to succeed. Incompatibilities need to be negotiated thoughtfully. Not always easy when one partner is an introvert and the other an extrovert, when one likes the beach and the other the mountains, or when one is a meat eater and the other is vegan.

All things being equal, coordination is a preferable strategy. Let's take a practical example to understand how coordination over compromise can be applied in real life. My friend Darwyn is like a brother, but there's an aspect of our lifestyles that is a challenge. He is a night owl, and I am an early bird. This limits the amount of time we can spend together and affects what we do, as he is often headed out for the evening as I climb into bed. In the design of our relationship, we rarely ask each other to compromise. It's great to go to the gym with him and dish between sets, but we gave that up years ago. Darwyn likes to work out at 8:00 p.m. I like to work out at 11:00 a.m. If we met in the middle, we would both be worse off. We coordinate schedules and pick activities that we can dedicate proper time and energy to.

After design, the next element is evaluation. Try out the early version of the relationship—the container—and see how it does.

I will share a story of compromise that survived the evaluation phase. My friend Christina was dating someone, and he suggested that she should get a more comfortable couch for her place. Christina wasn't entirely convinced, but she decided to try. She chose a couch from a company she liked; it wasn't her first choice in terms of style, but *wow* was that couch comfortable. As it turned out, the new couch provided a more relaxing space for hanging out and watching movies. It added value to their relationship. (Her dog, Snoop, also liked the couch). The relationship ended, but she still owns what she fondly calls her "compromise couch."

The final design step is to iterate—come full circle and revisit the agreement, adjusting and solidifying the container along the way. It is often enough to just ask, "How are you feeling about the relationship?" or "How do you think things are going?" or "Is there any part of our agreement that you want to revise?" Parties may renegotiate and redefine the boundaries and characteristics of their relationships as needed. Thus, they may have a different container moving forward. This purposeful crafting of relationships, instead of passively accepting societal norms, allows for more fulfilling and authentic connections.

Negotiating wants and needs is a cornerstone of any relationship. However, disagreements are inevitable. So, what happens if parties cannot come to an agreement? Is that the end of the relationship? Maybe, in the case of "deal breakers." For example, if a romantic partner must merge lives with me, we are not going to move forward. For non–deal breakers, relationship design can help people create a different container than they have with someone else. Suppose I met someone who would want a merged life but doesn't need one—we could explore having a romantic relationship, while she seeks a different partner for cohabitation. That may seem far-fetched, but people do it.

Jessicka Chamberlain (aka Joosey) appeared on the *Solo* podcast to teach me about relationship anarchy. Joosey refers to herself as "single but highly occupied." She has used design principles to incorporate a "comet"—a partner who comes in her life on rare occasions—into her repertoire of relationships. Whether or not she is dating someone else, Joosey's "comet" will join her in Las Vegas. They have a blast playing craps, going to the spa, and flirting with women. Sometimes, someone Joosey is seeing joins them as well. This may earn some puzzling looks and sideways glances (even in Vegas), but Joosey thinks the situation is ideal. "Throwing out the rules makes it a lot easier for me to listen to the relationship because the rules aren't distracting me from what the relationship should or shouldn't be."

Imagine feeling that free in love and life.

Let's look at practical examples of how relationship design can be used to cocreate:

- *Friendship negotiation:* Maxine has a friend with whom she enjoys spending time, but her friend has a full schedule and an ambitious career. Maxine decides to use relationship design to broach the topic over coffee, telling her friend that she would like to explore socializing more often. Her friend is flattered and acknowledges that it might be difficult, but they agree to explore by setting up a recurring fun night out together each week. After a few weeks, this turns out to be too taxing, and they revisit the agreement. Now, they have one fun night every other week, and cowork together on the alternate weeks.

- *Managing lifestyle expectations:* Jake is an aspiring professional bodybuilder who prioritizes his physical health. He begins dating Thomas, who likes to go out for cocktails, an activity that isn't compatible with Jake's regimented lifestyle. Rather than break up, Jake decides to have an open conversation and proposes some limitations on when and how they see each other. The couple can have healthy nights-in once or twice a week, and Thomas can go out with other friends to get his party fix.

- *Introducing nonhierarchy:* While the relationship escalator crowds out relationships that are not romantic and sexual,

platonic partners Tina and Tracy decide that their romantic partners do not have "veto power" over their friendship.
Each has a design conversation that results in not needing
to ask permission from their respective romantic partners
when planning social events, vacationing together, or
spending holidays with each other's families.

- *Relationship hiatus:* Pat and Celeste start dating casually and
have a promising connection. However, Celeste has a
major work project that is going to crowd out her social
life; she is launching a new product in two months. They
discuss this challenge openly and decide to temporarily
pause their relationship and revisit with a date to celebrate
after she finishes the launch.

- *Seeking arrangements:* Regardless of what you think of the
growing world of "arrangements" between a sugar baby
and sugar daddy/mommy, these partnerships often follow
relationship design principles as the parties negotiate their
wants and expectations from the outset. The parties discuss
financial support, emotional connection, and companionship preferences, revising as necessary. For example, they
may start with an agreement of four or five public dates a
month with an allowance for the "baby" and revise as
needed.

As we've seen with the above cases, relationship design allows
for creativity and flexibility in catering to the unique needs and
preferences of the people involved. Whether it's negotiating
time spent with a friend, accommodating lifestyle differences, or
navigating nontraditional relationship structures, the central
theme is open communication and willingness to adapt.

Given the potential of relationship design, it's crucial to
address the challenges involved. Navigating the nuance of

relationship design requires excellent communications skills, but like most worthwhile endeavors, the effort invested can yield deeply fulfilling relationships. As you experiment with the process, you will find that few people have experience explicitly designing a relationship. If you aim for a collaborative process where you depart from societal norms, partners who are unfamiliar with relationship design or its equivalents will need to be guided through this paradigm shift. In my experience, showing that you want to invest in a relationship with someone is a great way to show relationship design is better than *not* talking about the relationship. If a potential relationship partner won't give it a try, that person may not be a good match.

Relationship design involves cooperative negotiation. It's important to communicate your desires, but also crucial to be receptive and understanding if a partner has differing views. Relationship design isn't a competition with winners and losers; it's about collaboratively crafting a dynamic that serves the well-being of all involved. This process demands a willingness to be vulnerable and open to the possibility that the relationship might not align with both parties' values and goals. Engaging in relationship design may sometimes lead to the end of what might have seemed like a promising connection. For instance, my experience has shown that when a would-be partner who wants kids learns I have a vasectomy, things may end amicably or, better yet, morph into a professional connection, friendship, or even a sexual friendship. In such cases, it's essential to recognize that a sense of self-sufficiency, comfort in one's own skin, and confidence in unconventional choices—pillars of Solohood—form the foundation for a relationship design.

You might think this sounds exhausting. Yes, it is more work than defaulting into an ill-fitting agreement. I think it is for the best, but all this talking and negotiating may be discouraging (compared to the norm of defaulting and not talking). I suggest starting by asking for what you want and look for simple yes-no responses. Then, you can lay out things slowly and enjoy the relationship in the meantime, continually building and negotiating as you get more comfortable.

## DESIGNING YOUR SEX LIFE

Intimacy design is a special case of relationship design intended to enhance sexual experiences. Whether you're embarking on your first sexual encounter or getting spicy to celebrate a golden wedding anniversary, intimacy design can improve your sex life by fostering safer and more fulfilling encounters.

**Intimacy design is an intentional act of cocreating a customized sexual experience—prior to and perhaps during sex—where all involved parties create mutual agreements and make it a point to regularly review and revise the agreements as necessary.**

The process can improve sex and sensuality by way of conversation, planning, and consent. It has little to do with the movie trope of lovers, hot and heavy, spontaneously ripping off each other's clothes and making passionate love. Intimacy design is a thoughtful cocreation process that will require reimagining how to approach sexual relationships.

Recall the three magical design words: Prototype, Evaluate, and Iterate. Now, apply this to bumping uglies.

A good place to start an intimacy design practice is to talk about sexually transmitted infections (STIs), testing, and safe sex, so you and your partners can make informed decisions. This would entail disclosing the date of your last test, what was tested for, and the results. Present any history of infections, past or current, and any pertinent health vulnerabilities. Discuss STIs and pregnancy protections that are in place or expected, such as the use of preventive medications (e.g., PrEP) and/or barriers (e.g., condoms).

Once those topics are discussed, the next step is to communicate desires, boundaries, and consent with your partners (a sexual container of sorts). It is also important to create an atmosphere where all partners feel safe and respected during these discussions. I like to have this conversation prior to things becoming intimate—on the couch or over dessert rather than in the bedroom.

A good starting point is to ask partners about how they are feeling. Are they comfortable, excited, tired, nervous? Encourage all parties involved to volunteer what they are looking for and what they are not looking for. One way to approach this conversation it is to seek a "Yes," "No," or "Maybe" response. Establish "No" as a welcomed answer, because you can steer clear of something that makes your partner uncomfortable. "Maybe" requires further exploration and clarification for it to become a "Yes" or "No." When in doubt, "Maybe" means "No."

Here are examples of statements that can be used during the design conversation to communicate desires, boundaries, and establish consent:

- "When I come over, I would like you to greet me with a big hug and kiss. Is that in line with how you would like us to greet each other?"
- "I am really excited to see you, but I am feeling low energy tonight. I could rally to give you the full fireworks if that is

important to you, but if you are okay with it, I would be happy if we could have an old-school, run-of-the-mill shag."
- "I would like us both to wash our hands before we get naughty."
- "I would like you to use the restraints on me tonight. Are you game?"

The overall goal is to find eager consent, with a resounding "Yes" from all parties.

It is crucial to recognize that comfort levels and desires can evolve over time. The design conversation should be revisited periodically, and both partners should be open to the possibility that "Yes," "No," or "Maybe" could change depending on various factors.

There are obvious challenges of intimacy design:

- *Teaching it to your partners*: You may need to introduce and explain intimacy design to your partners. From my experience, it is often greatly appreciated as a refreshing approach to an experience that can be especially fraught early on.
- *Vulnerability and honesty*: Ask for what you want, but don't expect to always get what you want. You might not always be able to reach an agreement. But as a Solo, your experiences have likely taught you the power of vulnerability. It's through being vulnerable that we connect more deeply with others, even when it comes to the delicate matter of intimacy.
- *Respect others' preferences*: It is important not to "yuck someone else's yum." Just because you might not be into a certain act or scenario doesn't mean it's wrong or invalid. Also

avoid coaxing and cajoling. No means no. It is not okay to coax unless a partner has explicitly expressed that they want that kind of experience.

- *Sobriety*: Intimacy design is most effective when sober. This is because clear communication and consent are central to intimacy design, and these are both compromised when under the influence.

All this talking and planning may strike you as decidedly unsexy. I contend, however, that when done right, the agreement can build anticipation, remove anxiety, and ensure consent.

And consent is sexy.

## DESIGNING A BREAKUP

Just as a relationship can take a designed hiatus (à la Pat and Celeste), the end of a relationship can also be planned and structured thoughtfully. Sometimes ties must be completely severed, such as in the case of abuse or dishonesty. However, many times, relationships can be adapted or reinvented, which is particularly challenging to conventional relationship expectations.

Whether navigating a casual dating breakup or a contentious divorce, the end of a romance often follows predictable scripts: sadness, acrimony, and feelings of failure. In contrast, Gwyneth Paltrow popularized the term "conscious uncoupling," which was developed by psychotherapist Katherine Woodward Thomas in her 2011 book with the same title. Conscious uncoupling is one approach to ending romantic relationships with mutual respect and consideration for a partner's emotional well-being.

Relationship design offers a constructive way to not sunset but redefine a relationship in ways that reduce conflict, and perhaps, allow a new connection to emerge. A powerful example of taking an alternative approach comes from twenty-seven-year-old Monique Murad, a proud member of the Solo community and guest on my podcast. Monique describes her divorce as "joyful and celebratory." She and her husband chose to approach the dissolution of their marriage with love and intention, treating each other with respect and kindness throughout the process. Monique explained to me, "We held onto that until the end. . . . We were also full of joy at the work that we put in." They remain friends.

Instead of uncoupling, relationship design can be used to figure out how to redefine the relationship without the acrimony and perhaps even without a divorce or breakup. Partners can collaboratively address their mismatched goals or lifestyles and reshape the relationship container to accommodate individual needs. For example, partners might decide to sleep in separate bedrooms or live in different cities while still maintaining a connection. Or they may decide to make the relationship nonmonogamous or turn it into a platonic co-parenting partnership.

**Breaking rules is hard. Creating something new is harder.**

Applying relationship design principles to creating or sunsetting a relationship has nontrivial challenges and potential for failure. Yet, failure rates in relationships are already sky high.

Embracing the pillars of Solohood acknowledges your independence and the power you have in defining your relationships. Experimenting with relationship design is a testament to your self-sufficiency, your willingness to be vulnerable, and your confidence in taking a road that few have traveled.

Try, assess, and try again.

## SOLO LOVE LETTER

### Robert, CEO/Coach, Colorado, USA

Two years ago, I made the decision to divorce my wife and set up a new life for myself. I had reached a point of understanding that "the way" was never going to work for us. There's a lot to unpack in this, and I don't want people to think this was simple and unemotional. It was *hell*. I didn't want to divorce, but I found a point where it was the only way I personally could move forward.

In that process, I was extremely lucky to develop a "Solo" mindset. It allowed me to take ownership over my experiences. I began a process of living that empowered me to value my personal experience and to have healthy boundaries. Hearing others' stories and extrapolating data from the Solo movement helped me create a model for working through my divorce. I knew my goal was to not lose myself to depression and to use the new life I had been given as an opportunity for awakening.

I then intentionally designed how I wanted my divorce to look and built a strong co-parenting relationship and post-divorce relationship with my ex. I have found that, for me, being married is not the goal anymore. I could see that "the way" we are supposed to live is limited to one belief system that cannot be "the way" for all of us. I had to work through shame, anger, frustration, and a sense of judgment to find peace with the empowerment I now feel.

I was able to see worth in my life beyond being a provider and felt the necessity to not feel beholden to the system that culture had built around me. I remember immediately feeling free after starting the divorce process. Yes, I felt pain, betrayal, sadness, but I also felt free. I cannot express the value of that one feeling in comparison to the rest. Solo helped me see ways of using that freedom for exploration and personal growth. The Solo community also makes me not feel alone. I want "Solo" to become a mindset or philosophy that we teach our kids as I now teach my daughter. I want us all to see our choice in the lives we live. My goal is to be Solo: Connected and Free.

## SOLO LOVE LETTER

**Monique, Social Impact Consultant, Rio de Janeiro, Brazil**

I am twenty-seven, happily divorced, and living in Rio de Janeiro, Brazil. I love to dance, to climb, swim in the ocean, and, most important, spend time with my people. I have family and friends spread out all over the world. I identify as Solo, but am far from alone.

I met my former partner at eighteen, got married at twenty-three, and am now separated and in the process of getting divorced. When I look at this trajectory, I think, I was happily dating at eighteen, got happily married at twenty-three, and, though not an easy journey, am happily divorced at twenty-seven. When I say "happily," I mean I was and am extremely fulfilled by each of these decisions I made, based on the values and goals I had at the time. Each phase came with its ups and downs, the easy and the difficult. But the part of the journey that I felt the most shame in wanting to depart from was the divorce. So my partner and I decided to take a turn, to recognize the hard, and celebrate the good. Not all days are easy, but celebrating something is a choice, something we choose every day. If the choice to get divorced was what was best for both of us, liberating us to salvage the best parts of our relationship and redefine our future together, why can't I say we are happily doing so? I am privileged to have the financial and social freedom to be able to recognize that being in a marriage, in the more traditional sense, was not working for me, and work through the shame to find a dynamic that will serve me. This is where I identify what is mine by choice.

*Mine by choice.* Single, to me, didn't and doesn't fit the bill for my current stage of life. I like to say I am now and forever "my own" by choice. This means I belong to no one but myself, and no lover or friend belongs to me. I may have dependencies in my life, with lovers, with friends, with family, even with work, where I am needed, where I need them, but I make these choices so that my body, my mind, my life, is still my own to navigate.

I would say I am actively dating . . . myself, lovers, and friends. I identify with ways of living that value different relationships equally. I am actively investing in my family, friends, and romantic relationships by prioritizing them, not by these categories. My goals now are to invest in relationship dynamics that create healthy dependencies, but I will never again belong to anyone but myself.

# TEN

# A Model for a Remarkable Life

N early thirty years ago, I met Lisa Slavid in a little corner of paradise. I had just moved from New Jersey to Santa Barbara, California, seeking an escape from a lifetime of Jersey living. Fine for many, including my delightful sister, but not me. I dreamed of exploring the world. The American West. The Great Wall of China. The Pyramids of Giza. Though I wasn't yet a self-proclaimed Solo, I already felt the tug of a core tenet of the Solo philosophy. I wanted to lead a remarkable life. That desire, which unites all Solos from *Just May* to *No Way*, connected me with a fellow kindred spirit who was also adjusting to life in Southern California.

Lisa and I bonded while finding our footing in this new environment. In our first real job, we were hall directors at the University of California, Santa Barbara. We were tasked with organizing chaos: twenty-five staff members and four hundred first-year students in our respective dormitories. In our special way, we both got our fill of parenting.

These were angsty times. To cope, we would go on long beach walks and make David Letterman–inspired top ten lists of "things that don't suck." As my first friend who was both Jewish and a lesbian, Lisa—who affectionately referred to me as her "big dumb guy" friend—taught me new perspectives, especially about women. She was a good person and a good friend.

At some point during our walks, Lisa would break off to draw by the beach. I would go play basketball. Our lives also took different paths. I left Santa Barbara to pursue my PhD at Ohio State, while Lisa stayed and climbed the student affairs ladder to a director-level position. We both took breaks to work on Semester at Sea, a travel-abroad program where you take a sail around the world. (I succeeded in my quest to walk the Great Wall and see the sunrise at the Pyramids.) I watched proudly from afar as she turned her artistic skills into a successful series of charming, single-pane cartoons called *Peadoodles*.

We have since been reunited as Solos.

Lisa had an escalator partner for a while, but she has spent most of her life single and developing the Solo pillars of completeness, self-sufficiency, and unconventionality.

As age fifty approached, Lisa was sensing friction in her life (middle age will do that to you). A health scare led her to reflect on her accomplishments and contemplate what she still wanted to achieve in life. This is akin to facing a "second mountain." Climbing a second mountain is an exciting but challenging endeavor. The idea behind a second mountain is that, once you have made it to the top of a mountain—garnered a secure job at a university, for example—it is difficult but enriching to start anew. Facing another long, uncertain climb, there's the potential for a higher peak.

A second mountain may entail new professional challenges, new hobbies, new friends, a new locale, a divorce, or all of the above.

**FIGURE 6:** Lisa's Second Mountain care of *Peadoodles* (2020).

Lisa curtailed her work hours (and salary) to focus more on her art and consulting business. She wanted the freedom to do more of what she wanted to do on her own terms rather than within the hierarchy of a university. This trial run turned into her decision to retire early from her job on a half pension. This was no easy decision to retire early, but it was fueled by a desire for personal fulfillment and adventure. She got her financial house in order, downsized her living situation, picked up a roommate, and experimented with being a digital nomad while maintaining her Santa Barbara home base.

I don't know how Lisa's climb will turn out. I can tell you she is living a richer life with more independence than before. She could have easily stayed in her job for another fifteen or twenty years and increased her pension, but instead she gets to take this chance while she is still young (and, yes, I do think fifty is young).

Lisa's remarkable adventure exploring the limits of her artistic and entrepreneurial abilities may not appeal to you. But that's the beauty of it—there are endless paths to take. For instance, someone might find fulfillment in dedicating themselves to a cause, becoming an activist, or starting a family later in life. There is more than one remarkable life. There are remarkable lives. To copy Lisa's life would be a mistake, just as it would be to live your life to make Aunt Sally happy. A remarkable life is about how you feel about the way you spend your time.

If you want a reinvention, a second mountain, whatever you want to call it, it helps to have a model of well-being with whom to consult.

Stetson off. Professor hat on.

Abraham Maslow's hierarchy of needs is taught in introductory psychology classes and discussed at cocktail parties around the world. Maslow posits that people pursue basic (physiological and safety) needs, and if successful, progress toward higher-order needs. Next are psychological needs (belonging/love/prestige/achievement). At the highest level is self-actualization, where people, having met their basic needs, focus on personal growth, creativity, and reaching their true potential.*

Despite its popularity, usefulness, and intuitive appeal, Maslow's model has imperfections that subsequent models of well-being attempted to address.

---

* It is interesting that Maslow never conceptualized the model as a pyramid. Some management consultants in the 1960s did that.

Maslow put too much emphasis on hierarchy. Beyond taking care of basic needs, the need to maintain all previous steps in order to advance doesn't hold up to scrutiny. People could be living their best life devoid of prestige, even social connections (essential elements to reach actualization in Maslow's model). Consider the lone wolf painter compelled to create in isolation in her damp studio, day in, day out. She may never experience fame (or perhaps it will happen posthumously), but still can be living her best life.

For Solos, especially, the model does not adequately capture the diversity of experiences within a person, across people, and across cultures. What constitutes a good life in the United States versus Korea versus Nigeria? Having a single climb up the hierarchy is too limiting and fails to describe the many paths one can take to a remarkable life. The top of the metaphorical pyramid depends on the person. A model that describes how people live remarkably needs to accommodate differences in people's desires and what they consider to be a good life at age twenty or fifty or eighty.

My postdoctoral training was with Daniel Kahneman, a Nobel Prize winner who was deeply immersed in the topic of well-being when I arrived at Princeton to work with him. I was particularly drawn to this topic as it is a question that great philosophers have puzzled over for millennia. Danny let me share his office; we could work more closely when he was on campus. In our conversations, I found myself reflecting on my own journey and questioning the existing research.

The next generation of models were better than Maslow's in some ways and worse in others. The research identified two paths to well-being: One is a life of positive emotions. A life of physical pleasures and emotional joys: laughs, ease, tasty meals, restful night's sleep, sex—whatever it may be. The other is a life of meaning. People are often compelled to do something challenging to help others. Meaningful efforts such as raising children, curing cancer, or getting people to vote may be satisfying to accomplish, but often require a trade-off, sacrificing positive emotions.

These new models seemed too limiting to me—in part because I was so satisfied with my life, yet my life didn't fit their prescriptions. My life wasn't that pleasurable or particularly meaningful (yet). Nevertheless, I was living remarkably, in my opinion. And that is the only opinion that matters.

I wanted to develop my own model. Conversations with Danny drove me to delve into the work of Martin Seligman, one of the fathers of the positive psychology movement. His research highlights how well-being is not a one-size-fits-all concept. There were more layers, more textures than just pleasure and meaning. His research expanded the paths to a remarkable life. Some people want to cure cancer, others want to become billionaires, and others want to dedicate themselves to a monastic life. Some people will leave behind those endeavors to start a family, while others will bounce between worlds. Seligman's work is a major ingredient in the model that I developed. In his book *Flourish*, Seligman presents five paths that he labels PERMA: Positive emotion (P), Engagement (E), Relationships (R), Meaning (M), and Achievement (A).

The other ingredient was provided by Scott Barry Kaufman, a psychologist and author of *Transcend: The New Science of Self-Actualization*. He revises Maslow's theory by expanding its scope to account for various paths to well-being.

Scott introduces a sailboat metaphor. The brilliance of the sailboat metaphor lies in its ability to accommodate the versatility and autonomy of the individual, solving a major problem with Maslow's hierarchy. A key element of the sailboat metaphor is people's ability to chart a course in any direction. To do that, they need a sturdy hull to prevent the boat from capsizing in rough waters, and a large sail to catch wind and move swiftly through the seas (though sometimes the sail is down, as is the case with an illness, loss of a job, or heartbreak).

Now picture an ocean with billions of sailboats, some bobbing along, others catching wind, and yet others, unfortunately, capsized.

## THE FOUNDATION-FLOURISH MODEL

Inspired by Maslow's idea that there are basic needs to take care of before moving on to higher-order goals, the Foundation-Flourish model is my way to think about living a remarkable life. Scott and I have different elements for the hull (what he calls safety) and the sail (which he calls growth). I refer to them as *foundation* and *flourishing*, respectively.

## FOUNDATION

A solid foundation in life occurs for people fortunate enough to have solidified their health, wealth, and community, which serve as a sturdy hull:

1.  *Health:* Physical and mental well-being are crucial to living a remarkable life. A solid foundation includes a better approach to sleeping, eating, and moving. Perhaps also doing the hard work to address chronic pain, addiction, trauma, and associated mental health issues.
2.  *Wealth:* Financial stability is essential, especially for singles. Being out of debt with a steady income provides freedom to pursue your passions and interests. To get there,

reduce unnecessary expenses, begin saving, and invest in your future self. Note: Don't actually buy a sailboat.

3. *Community:* Study after study demonstrates social connections are one of the best predictors of well-being. Finding "the one" is not the only way, however. Nurturing healthy relationships with family, friends, and colleagues is a key aspect of a firm foundation. Building a strong support network—big or small—is essential to counteracting the risks of going it alone.

The 2009 World Happiness Report authored by John Helliwell and colleagues used data from the World Values Survey and other sources to examine well-being in countries around the world. The researchers found that six factors explained 75 percent of the variance in well-being. Four were related to the foundational elements: 1) Healthy life expectancy, emphasizing the value of good health; 2) GDP per capita, illustrating the role of wealth; 3) Freedom to make life choices, reinforcing wealth's influence; 4) Social support, signifying the importance of community; 5) Generosity; and 6) Perceptions of corruption.

Life is fraught with challenges and unforeseen obstacles. Establishing a solid foundation in terms of health, wealth, and community is no small feat. For many people, the foundational elements of their lives capture most of their attention.

## FLOURISH

A big sail is present to the degree someone is living a life of purpose, engagement, and/or positive emotion. With a foundation in place, Solos can focus on embracing an identity and associated activities of the artist, athlete, scientist, entrepreneur, volunteer, public servant, cool aunt or uncle, or any number of roles related to purpose, creativity, or pleasure.

1. *Purpose:* Pursuing a challenge bigger than oneself is a hallmark of a remarkable, purposeful life. Purpose has two categories: 1) meaning: serving or doing something bigger than yourself for others (e.g., adopting a child, volunteering at a homeless shelter, contributing to the Solo movement); or 2) achievement: creating something bigger than yourself for yourself (e.g., building a business, winning an Oscar, running your first or fiftieth marathon).

2. *Engagement:* A remarkable life may be one of creative pursuits that capture your interest and immerse you in a state of flow. Engaging in activities related to art, science, or business—things that require problem-solving and creativity—can bring a sense of satisfaction.

3. *Positive Emotion:* Cultivating happiness and other positive emotions is both personally rewarding and can uplift those around us. A remarkable life does not have to be all striving and struggle; it can be enjoyed.

The paths people take toward flourishing may change over time. What is a remarkable life at age twenty might not be so at age fifty or eighty. Even escalator riders may shift their focus, for example, from their partner to their children and back to their partner after their children leave the nest.

The same activity can help people flourish in different ways. For instance, learning to cook can be used to bring together community or help feed people at a homeless shelter (meaning), or open a Michelin star restaurant (achievement), or create a delightful meal (positive emotions), or create a flow-inducing creative challenge (engagement).

Pursuing a life of purpose, creativity, and pleasure all at the same time is exhausting. However, the paths aren't mutually exclusive. The same activity can check multiple boxes. For example, the Tough Mudder, an endurance challenge involving a ten- to twelve-mile obstacle course, could be achievement-focused while also being done for charity (i.e., meaning). Launching a business might be achievement-focused, but it can also be an engaging creative endeavor. Similarly, volunteering at an animal shelter can be emotionally fulfilling, bringing positive emotions through the joy of helping animals, while also serving a higher purpose by contributing to the welfare of the community.

I mix my metaphors too often. Lisa is climbing a second mountain, and Solos are captain of their own sailboat. Now, I ask you to become a shipbuilder and fashion a strong hull. Let's get to building in the next two chapters.

## SOLO LOVE LETTER

### Jordan, Equality, Diversity, Inclusion, and Well-Being Lead, London, UK

I became single in 2014 after finally leaving my abusive boyfriend of four years and the company I helped him run. At age twenty-eight, prime time for engagements, house purchases, and career successes among my peers, I found myself without a partner, job, income, or home, and with severely diminished self-esteem and mental health.

I immediately set about indulging in all that hookup apps and London's drinking culture have to offer someone in their twenties. This period was fun, life-affirming, and gave me a sense of freedom that I hadn't experienced during my years with a controlling partner. But, over time, the regular hangovers, repetitive dating chat, and creeping weight gain from all the alcohol and associated poor food decisions began to seem less fun and not worth the time or money they were consuming. I realized I needed to begin living intentionally, so I improved my diet, deleted the apps, and started exercising, volunteering, attending counseling, and broadening my social circle. I began the transition from single to Solo.

Two years and more counseling later, I had a new job, more friends, joined the board of a charity, completed a half marathon, and began studying part-time for a master's degree, a long-held dream of mine. I felt my life had been derailed by my abusive relationship, and I had now not only "caught up" to where it would have been, but was growing beyond that point into a new, more remarkable version of myself; one who takes steps to make her dreams happen.

## SOLO LOVE LETTER

### Angela, Communications Officer, Baltimore, Maryland, USA

I think I was always Solo at heart, without knowing it. I say "without knowing it" because there was no positive representation for that kind of life in the media or in my family. My parents lamented over a forever single/childless uncle, and I never knew why because to me he was *the best*.

One day, after being miserable and confused on my couch about my lot in life as an older single woman, a switch flipped. Most of the reason I was upset was because of societal expectations, not my own desires. I remembered how free I liked to feel in my twenties, which is why I resisted relationships; I didn't want to limit life's opportunities for me. I dove headfirst into the content of Bella DePaulo, Shani

Silver, Lucy Meggeson, and Peter McGraw. I planned what my great single life might look like, even if I wasn't committed to being single forever.

Then the pandemic happened.

I gave up drinking (I wasn't a heavy drinker but I feel so much healthier without it), got into Buddhist thinking (especially Pema Chödrön), started doing art (I'm pretty good for not having much training). I was very happy with my life.

My main issues with Solohood are that (i) my parents are worried about me and sad about no grandchildren (my sister didn't want kids forever; I was the only hope); and (ii) I'd love to split my rent. However, most people my age aren't looking for roommates. I'm hoping for a Golden Girls house once everyone starts getting divorced. I'd "manifest" one if I believed in that. And to be honest, it doesn't make sense for me to live with a romantic/sexual partner. What makes romance and sex exciting is often the longing and mystery. I couldn't imagine the romance and sexual tension remaining if I lived with a partner. Friendships for me are more stable in terms of affection, and I'd love to have daily morning coffee conversations with friend(s) rather than a romantic partner.

# ELEVEN

# Foundation

Lao Tzu's wise words "The journey of a thousand miles begins with a single step" are a reminder that building a solid foundation as a Solo is a journey. Small, consistent steps build the health, wealth, and community that are essential for self-sufficiency and launching point to flourishing. These are the three legs of a tripod—each one foundational in their own right. With all three in place, you can face life's challenges with poise and grace.

For Solos, foundation is paramount. Building a foundation not only liberates you from dependency on a partner but also instills confidence and resilience. It's important to acknowledge that people have different circumstances and privileges, so the journey will vary for each person. While I am no expert, my intention is to inspire action toward building a strong foundation.

So, let's lace up our metaphorical walking shoes and embark on this empowering journey toward vigor, prosperity, and connection. Oh, and as you will see, there will be literal steps too.

· · ·

## VIGOR

"A healthy person wants a thousand things. A sick person wants one thing." This adage reveals the essential role of health; it is the bedrock upon which all other aspirations are built.

My parents faced immense health struggles. My mom was proud and tenacious, but battled poor health, especially in her final years. She dealt with mental illness, chronic pain, and piercing loneliness. She died at sixty-nine. My dad was quiet and kind. However, his untamed nature led him to make choices that took a toll on his health. He was addicted to cigarettes, drank too much, didn't exercise, and the only meal I witnessed him prepare was a homemade Philly cheesesteak. He died of cancer at age fifty-four.

Whenever I am struggling with life, I ask, "Is my health number one?" This question is a call to action. My parents' stories underline the essence of health in the Solo's journey. Their experiences serve as a poignant reminder that, without our health, we miss out on the joys of life and become dependent on others. Investing in health empowers Solos to be self-sufficient, confident, and resilient. Plus, it feels good.

With that said, I am not a health professional. I cannot dispense health advice. You will need to lean on the pros. But I can offer encouragement. So, here we go.

## REST AND RECOVERY

Is your sleep number one?

Danny Kahneman would quip that you can ask someone how happy they are or you can ask them how well they have been sleeping. You sleep better when life is good, and life is good when you sleep better. Indeed, sleep is a superpower essential for mental, physical, and emotional well-being.

*Prioritizing sleep.* In embracing the Solo lifestyle, rest and recovery hold particular significance. Both the quality and quantity of sleep play a crucial role in emotion regulation, cognitive function, and physical health. Your goal is to get seven to nine hours of high-quality sleep. Start by establishing a consistent sleep schedule, even on weekends. My pro tip is to schedule sleep the same way you schedule work or a dentist appointment.

*Creating a sleep-friendly environment.* Start by silencing the sounds in your bedroom, picking the perfect temp, and dialing down the lights. The darker the room, the better. I use a sleep mask to help with that endeavor. Don't skimp on the cushy stuff: a comfortable mattress and pillows that fit your sleeping style. Finally, remove your TV from the room—and your (damn) phone. After all, your bed should be a haven exclusively for two "S-related" activities: snoozing and snuggling.

*Winding down.* It's not just the time in bed that matters, either. The time before also matters. I use the 3-2-1 rule for winding down. Three hours before bed, I stop eating (this rule also helps if you are susceptible to late-night bingeing). Two hours before bed, I limit water intake to prevent stumbling around at 4:00 a.m. to pee. One hour before bed, I turn off all screens and digital devices. I go analog: vinyl, journals, notepads, books, and stretching. Perhaps I am putting you to sleep, which would make me happy.

Being tired is an acute state of fatigue that can be remedied by a couple good nights of sleep. Being worn out, on the other hand, is a chronic state of fatigue that requires more than sleep to recover from. It requires extended periods of rest and recovery to bounce back (and may require the involvement of a healthcare provider). Sometimes you don't even know what non–worn out life can be like, because humans are so good at convincing themselves that feeling like crap is "normal." That's no way to live.

A vacation is a good start—especially a long one in nature. Research shows that time in natural environments reduces stress, lowers blood pressure, and improves mood. When was the last time you walked barefoot in grass or sand? Swam in a lake? Walked through a dense forest?

## Resting your mind

Imagine Jerry Seinfeld, legs crossed, eyes closed, in deep meditation. As laughable as that may seem, the comedy icon has been practicing meditation since the 1970s. While others would go to lunch during the taping of *Seinfeld,* he would meditate, which he attributes to surviving nine years of taxing work on one of the most popular sitcoms ever made.

Meditation is an ancient practice that trains your mind to be more present, better focused, and on less of a roller coaster. Brain scans show that Tibetan monks who practice hours of meditation a day have the happiest brains in the world. Meditation is difficult and takes practice to get good at it. It also helps to find the right kind of meditation. I am particular to *Loving-Kindness Meditation.* Spread the love far and wide by silently repeating well-wishes for yourself and others (even that annoying coworker who steals food from the office fridge). My loving-kindness practices have been helpful when academic colleagues criticize my intellectual pursuits.

## FUEL

Gone are the days of our hunter-gatherer and even our agrarian ancestors, who were preoccupied with obtaining enough food to survive. Today, the Western world now suffers from the opposite problem. Our concern has shifted from scarcity to navigating the complexities of too much food, too often, and not enough of the right kind. The risk of obesity is so profound that anything you can do to address weight struggles will have the greatest return on your investment of time, energy, money, and the sacrifice of mouth pleasure.

You may be bored by the thought of delving into food within a book about singles, but nutrition is a fundamental component of self-sufficiency. Being self-sufficient is not just about financial independence; it's also about taking care of your basic needs, and food is as basic as it gets. Can you prepare a healthy meal from real, unprocessed ingredients?

Stockpiling mac and cheese might be the quintessential bachelor joke, but there's truth in jest. I calculated that one summer break during college, I survived on three hundred peanut butter and jelly sandwiches. Eating actual foods, as opposed to overly processed stuff, has numerous benefits, including improved mood and energy levels. Moreover, people who frequently eat out tend to consume more calories and less nutritious food. So, for Solos who wish to build a foundation of self-reliance, learning to prepare and enjoy nourishing meals is essential.

To achieve a healthy balance of quality and quantity, it's important to consume nutrient-dense, whole foods while practicing portion control and mindful eating. I will finish with a word about alcohol: It is terrible for you and crazy expensive. If you are a drinker, strive to move your drinking from regular and mundane to rare and special. That is, if you drink, reserve it for special occasions, such as celebrating getting out of debt. If you don't drink, congratulations.

## MOVEMENT

Walking saved me. More than a dozen years ago, I was crisscrossing the globe doing research for my first book, teaching several classes, and hustling to publish research papers. Oh, and I had a girlfriend. I caught a virus that was nasty enough to slow me down, but not so nasty that I was bedridden. By the end of the day, all I could do was watch TV and eat nachos to cope, which made me feel even worse. The illness went on for weeks.

I was unhappy. One cold November night, I thought, *Enough.* I bundled up and went for a walk around my neighborhood. The fresh air and brisk movement made me feel a little better. I did it the next night, and the next, and the next. Soon enough, I was back to normal. I credit my daily walk, which I continue to this day.

Walking is an often overlooked but incredibly effective form of exercise. It's accessible, low-impact, and can easily be incorporated into daily routines, whether you're walking to work, taking a lunchtime stroll, or just bopping around your neighborhood.[1]

Walking is only half the solution. The other side is making your muscles work. Michael Joyner, a physician and researcher, says, "Move your body every day. Sometimes very hard." There is a world of barbells, bands, body weight exercises, and other functional movements that help metabolic health, weight loss, and combat age-related muscle loss (which goes by the scary name of sarcopenia). Building muscle is essential to maintain physical autonomy. Think of this as investing in your long-term independence. Note: Building muscle takes years—so be persistent and patient.

To get your heart rate up, work your way up to hard hikes, fast swims, cycling, rows, sprints, kickboxing, or group fitness classes that elevate your heart rate and leave you breathless in a good way. Then sprinkle in fun movement: tennis, yoga, Pilates, pickleball dance, rock climbing, paddleboarding, tai chi, or yard work. You can leverage these activities not only for physical health but also as a way to socialize.

Low energy, injured, or recovering from a hard workout? My friend Charlie Merrill taught me the "move with joy" workout. Simply pick light-to-moderate exercises that you find fun. Perhaps get outside to do it. Despite risks of skin cancer and aging, there is compelling evidence that modest sun exposure is vital for well-being. Vitamin D, synthesized through sun exposure, plays a crucial role in maintaining overall health.

By combining good nutrition and consistent exercise, you can parent yourself into your eighties and beyond. Take a moment to picture yourself thirty, forty, or even fifty years from now. What do you see? As you visualize your future, consider the potential risks that come with aging, such as an increased likelihood of falls. The stakes are high—broken hips, reduced mobility, and a plummeting quality of life all start with your habits years before. Start training for eighty. Onward!

## PROSPERITY

Money is an emotional topic. My struggles to create financial security took till my forties, and I must confess, a feeling of security often eludes me. In a world built for two, Solos face a winding path of challenges navigating wealth and personal finance.

The upside to money and singlehood: optionality. The mobility inherent in the Solo life presents ample opportunities; from embracing an adventurous side hustle to gallantly relocating for a dream job, without the need to juggle the wants and needs of a partner. Moreover, having full sovereignty over your financial choices spares you from waking up to find someone else liquidating your savings to pay off gambling or shopping debts.

Money won't solve all your problems, but it will solve your money problems. Take Anita Dhake, the "Thrifty Gal," for instance, who waved adieu to the daily grind in her thirties through intense investing and a pared-down lifestyle. Wise beyond her years, Dhake views money as a path to freedom. Money is freedom from bad romantic entanglements. Money is freedom from a negative living situation. A bank balance enables you to make changes in your living arrangements, perhaps to escape an unhealthy relationship or just enjoy more solitude. Money is a cushion from bad bosses, hostility, or unfairness at work. Having money gives you the confidence to stand up to inappropriate behavior or actions in the workplace and leave if needed.

Singles don't have the buffer of a partner's income, making it crucial to wield the financial lance with precision. Financial stability includes ensuring that you have access to an emergency fund, good food, health insurance, and a proper place to live— the basic elements of parenting yourself.

### Out of the Red and into the Black

Grab a sheet of paper or open a spreadsheet and create two columns. List your assets (e.g., a home's value, savings, car, stocks) in the first column, and your liabilities (e.g., credit card debt, student loans, mortgages, car payments, insurance) in the second. Subtract your liabilities from your assets, and you will know if your net worth is positive (in the black) or negative (in the red).

If you are in the red especially, the first task is to conquer high-cost debt. Focus on credit card debt and student loans by paying them off on time, above the minimums. Don't miss a payment; that wrecks your credit score, and the additional fees are a killer. For the best results, tackle debts with the highest interest rates first. Don't be afraid to give your creditors a call to see if they'll work with you to lower interest rates or provide other assistance. Be careful of scammy debt consolidators.

Once you get your revolving credit card debt under control, it's time to build an emergency fund. While most experts suggest saving six months' worth of expenses, as a single person, consider aiming for at least nine months' worth of take-home pay. This may seem like an ambitious goal, but without the financial buffer a partner can provide, it's a prudent investment for singles. Keep in mind, your emergency fund is for emergencies (hence the term). If you are tempted to dip into it for some fun in the sun, start a vacation fund.

Being single often entails unique financial considerations. For example, with the potential for more financial flexibility, singles can explore various avenues for income diversification or investments. However, singles also need to be more vigilant about expenses and savings, as they may not have the additional support that comes from a dual-income household. Speaking of expenses, some expenditures might seem innocuous but can cumulatively take a toll on your savings. For instance, frequent spending on alcohol, dining out, DoorDash, and $5 lattes adds up. Embrace the art of DIY; whether it's whipping up a meal or brewing your own coffee, this not only saves money but can also become an engaging hobby.

Be aware of the cultural and psychological forces that lead people to make bad purchase decisions. One is to keep up with the Joneses. Wanting a better car because someone else has a better car is a terrible reason to get a better car. Another psychological force at play is hedonic adaptation, which is the tendency of humans to quickly adapt to changes in their circumstances, particularly positive ones. This trait can be beneficial for coping with adverse events, but when it comes to positive changes, it leads to a phenomenon known as the *hedonic treadmill.* Essentially, your situation improves, but your happiness levels don't see a corresponding increase. This is because you quickly adapt to the improvements and start seeking something even better. For example, you may be excited about a new car, but because of the hedonic treadmill, you will adapt to having it and start dreaming of a better car. Cars are incredibly expensive with additional costs—insurance, maintenance, parking, to name a few. If you can get away with walking, public transit, and rideshares, do it. But if you need a car, buy a reliable, economical used car and stop thinking that a new car will make you happier. It will, but only till the new car smell wears off.

Last, it's worth examining the cultural pressure of homeownership. While owning a home is a part of the traditional American Dream, it's not necessarily the best option for everyone, especially singles. Homeownership comes with ongoing costs such as maintenance, insurance, and property taxes. Additionally, real estate doesn't always appreciate as much as other investments. Next, homeownership has tons of hidden costs, such as lawn care and busted water heaters. Singles also might find themselves with space they don't use often, like garages, guest rooms, and the extra his or her sink. Finally, the fixed costs of buying, selling, and outfitting a home are high.

Thus, you want to stay in it long enough to recoup those costs, which typically takes five-plus years.

There are increasing alternative housing options for singles, such as co-living, micro-units, and co-op housing, which can be more suitable and cost-effective than traditional homeownership. But I am biased. I love apartment living. And there is no shame in having roommates! If it is good enough for the Golden Girls, it could be good for you.

Saving money by reducing expenses is just half of the equation. The other half is to increase your income by asking for a raise, finding a new job, finding a side hustle, and investing for passive income. If you don't work at a job that provides a pension, it is important to invest in employer-sponsored and government retirement accounts like 401(k), Traditional IRA, or Roth IRA. The best predictor of retiring financially sound is to start early and save till it hurts.

## HAROLD POLLACK'S INDEX CARD

**H**arold Pollack, a professor at the University of Chicago, wrote what is now a famous index card with rules to follow to manage personal finances effectively (my additions are in *italics*):

1. Max your 401(k) or equivalent employee contribution.
2. Buy inexpensive, well-diversified mutual funds, such as Vanguard Target 20XX funds (*where XX is the year you will retire*).
3. Never buy or sell an individual security (i.e., stock). The person on the other side of the table knows more than you do about this stuff.
4. Save 20 percent of your money.

5. Pay your credit card balance in full every month.
6. Maximize tax-advantaged savings vehicles like Roth, SEP, and 529 accounts.
7. Pay attention to fees. Avoid actively managed funds.
8. Make financial advisors commit to a fiduciary standard.

Number eight is often overlooked. My financial planner, Amy Gibb, whom you may recognize from my podcast as "Money Amy," is a fee-based, certified financial planner who is committed to giving me advice that is in my best interest (i.e., fiduciary standard) because she's paid for her time, not by a percentage of my investments. Conflict of interest eliminated.

Find your Money Amy or call mine!

## CONNECTION

While singles may not have, or may not desire, "the one," successful singles cultivate a diverse and vibrant community, replete with more friends and greater involvement than their married counterparts.

The term "urban tribes" was coined by Ethan Watters to describe a kind of support network (kin by choice) he was witnessing among his friends. Members of the urban tribe were postponing traditional life milestones like marriage and parenthood. They were living remarkably among friends. His observation was later substantiated by a 2020 study in the *Journal of Social and Personal Relationships* by Elyakim Kislev, which demonstrated that singles who are content with their friendships are less inclined to pursue a romantic partner. The study suggested that fulfilling friendships can meet individuals' needs for emotional support, companionship, and social engagement, decreasing the need to find a romantic relationship.

Solos can allocate their time and energy to strengthening family bonds, cultivating meaningful friendships, and participating actively in community activities. A social support system can be made up of family, friends, romantic partners, colleagues, and members of the community, including clergy, fellow congregants, and neighbors. Additionally, a strong community may involve various professionals such as doctors, financial advisors, handypersons, and even a barber or stylist, who's not only good at shaping the outside of your head, but also at shaping the inside of your head.

Savvy Solos will turn to therapists or life coaches for guidance. My long-standing therapist, fondly referred to as The Poet due to his lineage tracing back to William Butler Yeats, has been an invaluable resource. A troubled relationship with my mother, along with the burden of being her sole caregiver from afar, was making me deeply unhappy. Fortunately, with the help of The Poet, I managed to work through these issues.

When seeking a therapist or life coach, it's essential to find someone you can trust and feel comfortable with. Understanding their specialization is crucial as therapists and coaches vary in their expertise and approaches. Don't hesitate to "shop around" for the right fit and ask about their methodology (checklists are appropriate here). However, be cautious; some therapists might unintentionally push the traditional narrative of relationships. It's important to find a professional who respects and supports your choice to live as a Solo and can offer guidance tailored to that lifestyle. Give them this book, if needed, so I can continue my Solo financial security.

## Remarkable Friends

In the twentieth century, the term "chosen family" gained prominence in the LGBTQ+ community, where individuals often built families based on shared values and experiences, especially when they faced rejection from biological families.

For both singles and those in relationships, a diverse social network of friends is crucial in fulfilling needs and desires. Reduce the pressure on any one person and maximize their fit by picking the right friend for the right activity. For example, you might have different friends to have fun with, get advice from, or commiserate with during difficult times. Julie is my former-neighbor-turned-dear-friend of nearly twenty years (she is also a frequent guest cohost on my podcast). After about twenty invites to attend game nights, Julie told me not to bother inviting her anymore. No problem. I will have my game nights without her, though she remains an ideal hiking partner.

I suggest that a remarkable friend can be defined by three essential qualities. First, the person brings value to your life, and vice versa. This encompasses affection, appeal, and mutual interest, ensuring that both people are better off with the other in their life. Second, a remarkable friend is reliable and trustworthy, consistently showing up when they say they will, and maintaining confidentiality when entrusted with your secrets. Last, a remarkable friend practices compersion (i.e., anti-jealousy). They celebrate your successes and commiserate in your failures. A frenemy, on the other hand, is jealous of your successes and celebrates your failures.

Friedrich Nietzsche believed that friendship plays a crucial role in self-development. Friends can know you better than you know yourself. He attributed this to two key factors:

- **Perspicacity**, or the ability to notice and understand things that are difficult and not obvious, enables friends to provide unique insights into your character and actions. Their distance from you allows them to observe aspects of your life that you may not notice yourself. They are close, but not too close.

- **Honesty** is the willingness of friends to share their observations with you, even observations that are unpopular or difficult to hear. Friends are not always polite; they are genuine and open with one another. This honesty can create challenging situations, such as when a friend starts dating a jerk.

Navigating these situations can be difficult, but a good friend strives to maintain a balance of being "lovingly close while remaining respectfully distant," as Nietzsche wrote.

Despite its prominence and importance, friendship in the United States is facing a concerning decline, particularly among men. When asked about the number of close friends, women have experienced a decline, with 10 percent now reporting no close friends. The pattern is worse for men. Only 15 percent of male respondents reported having ten or more friends, while the percentage of those with no close friends increased from 3 percent to 15 percent. Ugh.

Improving connections and building a thriving community takes work:

- *Be a Remarkable Friend:* The best way to get is to give what you want to receive. Enhance other people's lives, be high integrity, and practice anti-jealousy.

- *Welcome Vulnerability:* Building connections necessitates a level of openness and vulnerability. Express gratitude to people who make a difference in your life and be forthright in stating your intentions when you wish to be friends with someone. This echoes the Solo foundations of genuine connection and self-awareness.

- *Give Existing Relationships TLC:* Rekindle existing friendships by reaching out to old friends or repairing strained relationships. Reflect on your current connections and make an effort to nurture the positive ones while graciously parting ways with relationships that no longer serve you. Relationship design is especially useful here.

- *Be an Active Participant:* Say "yes" to invites and attend various events. If an event doesn't resonate with you, leave early. If the event is engaging, stay and immerse yourself in the experience.

- *Host Social Gatherings:* Be the initiator by hosting events, happy hours, or casual get-togethers like a game night or a bowling outing. Creating environments where people can interact informally helps in forming bonds. In my experience, people enjoy a good theme party.

- *Join in Groups and Workshops:* Participate in meetups, workshops, or clubs that align with your interests. Engage in activities you are passionate about, which will draw you closer to like-minded individuals.

- *Contribute through Mentorship or Volunteer:* Offer your time and expertise by engaging in mentorship programs or community service. (Or vice versa by asking someone to mentor you.) This not only helps in giving back but also connects you with diverse people.

Building relationships and cultivating a community is an enriching but delicate endeavor that requires both openness and vulnerability. By aligning this process with the core principles of Solo living, it creates meaningful, supportive networks that enhance people's lives.

As you get older, sometimes it's more difficult to make friends and you have to work on it more. Surrounding yourself with other wholehearted unconventionalists makes it easier to be one yourself.

A final unsung hero of the Solo's community is a pet. Of singles in the United States, 65 percent own a pet. Pet cans be indispensable parts of a healthy, full Solo life. Just ask all those happy cat ladies.

To delve deeper into the reasons for pet ownership, I conducted a survey of 250 pet owners—primarily dog and cat owners, both single and partnered. The respondents were asked about their reasons for pet ownership, their relationship with their pet, and the impact of the pet on their lifestyle. Some notable disparities emerged.

When asked about the main reason for keeping a pet, the choices included companionship, love/happiness, meaning/purpose, protection, and other. Interestingly, singles were more likely to opt for companionship (67 percent compared to 44 percent for partnered owners), while partnered owners gravitated more toward love/happiness (47 percent compared to 25 percent of singles). Singles were more likely to describe their pets as partners (80 percent vs. 63 percent of non-single owners), and 78 percent admitted that they would probably or definitely choose their pet over a potential partner.

Having set the hull of our ship with a strong foundation through health, wealth, and community building, it's now time to catch the winds in our sails. Let's explore how Solos can flourish and ride the waves of life.

## SOLO LOVE LETTER

### DJC, Sometimes Healthcare Marketing, Switzerland

I f only . . .

How many times have I heard that? "Oh, Danny, *if only* you could find someone and get married, you will be so happy." I've had more helpful dessert recommendations from a waiter than this advice from family and friends recommending their life to me.

I tried. I really did. Blind dates. Speed dates. But I failed to fit into this prescribed lifestyle. And years later, I am thankful that I didn't succumb. Maybe I was stubborn, or lucky, or finally ready. I took a leap to change my path. I quit my corporate job, moved to a quirky town in the Rocky Mountains, and published a music magazine. I was delightfully out of my comfort zone, professionally and personally surrounding myself with people who encouraged a belief system of "If you live the life you want, you will be happy."

Flash-forward years later. I am still Solo and proud of my remarkable life. I've dated wonderful women, have had my heart broken, and even broke a heart or two myself. My passport has stamps from countries I never knew existed and adventures that I hope would have made Anthony Bourdain proud. My WhatsApp contacts are diverse in so many ways, and I am a damn good photographer, guitarist, and certified yoga teacher. I started an NGO in West Africa, volunteered in a jungle doing gorilla conservation, and lived at a Spanish beach to improve my language skills and tan. I love my nieces, nephews, and godchildren. I'm a cherished son, brother, friend, confidant, and mentor. I am a value-add at a party.

Financially, I've saved diligently without the pressures often accompanying partnered life. Solo life permits me to take extended pauses from my sometimes healthcare marketing nine-to-five grind, whether to try new business ventures or simply spend significant time watching baseball games with my father. Solo life allows me to book a flight whenever I want, wherever I want. I have my network for deep discussions, support, and socializing, and yet, I feel strongly that being Solo has pushed me to acquire and maintain a rewarding set of relationships. I value connection immensely.

For me, being Solo is a feature of who I am. We all deserve a fulfilling journey regardless of our life's itinerary. I am genuinely glad for those who choose a path of marriage and/or children. And, I am confident I've grown and experienced life differently as a Solo, as I was meant to be.

If only everyone had the chance to chart their own remarkable life.

## SOLO LOVE LETTER

### Shahreen, Physician, Houston, Texas, USA

**B**eing Solo is the prioritization of our personal well-being, building our personal identity outside of any relationship, and striving to experience strength and tranquility within ourselves.

I grew up in a religious South Asian family where there was a strong emphasis on marriage. I stayed the course during my early adulthood. I became a physician, got married, and had two children. After sixteen years of union, my marriage came to an end. Although my divorce was amicable, it was also intensely painful.

After becoming single, I delved into the misadventures of the over-forty dating world. I learned that relationships alone cannot sustain us, and with time, I grew to be hopeful for a better and brighter future as a Solo. My freedom and desire to create a new life inspired me to develop myself more than I ever had. I approach each day with a sense of curiosity and optimism. I've taken up new hobbies and also picked up old ones. I started riding a bike for the first time in more than twenty years. I plan on traveling more, taking up ballroom dancing, and creating more art. Overall, becoming Solo has had a positive impact on my passion for life and all that it has to offer.

My beliefs about friendship also evolved. It was as though friends went from playing extras to playing strong supporting roles in the movie of life, and the intimacy I create with my friends is much more fulfilling. Friendship is now even more important to me than romantic connections, because it is friendship that builds the foundation of any personal relationship. When you can value people for who they are over the role they play, you can shed the role and still stay connected to another's essence. And that is a beautiful thing.

The trade-off to being Solo is that sometimes it can get lonely. But that loneliness can help us to strengthen ourselves and to also look beyond ourselves to strengthen our relationships. Loneliness can also inspire creativity, and I have found that my best ideas came to me during my periods of solitude.

Some say there is nothing like being in a relationship to help you grow. Some say there is nothing like being single to help you grow. I believe there is nothing like change to help you grow. So, whether it is embarking on a new relationship, tying the knot, experiencing the dissolution of a relationship, or facing the ever-changing seasons of partnered life or single life, one thing is for certain: You will grow. It is our commitment to our growth that allows us to do difficult things, to face our deepest fears, and to take risks. It is our commitment to our growth that truly empowers us.

# TWELVE

## Flourish

I n college, I stumbled into the Greek ethos, the pursuit of "*arete.*" In ancient Greek culture, arete represented the realization of one's fullest potential, encompassing excellence, virtue, and the best of one's character, both in mind and body. Think of the "scholar-athlete"—blending intellect and physical prowess.

I pursued a life in academia because I loved the intellectual vibrancy of university life. I also wanted a secure job. Academia is like government work—reliable pay and benefits if you make the cut—except you can't leave the office at 5:00 p.m. My twenties, thirties, and forties were populated by research papers, statistical analysis, and the thrill of scientific discoveries. Simultaneously, I would sneak out of the lab to build my body in the gym and compete on the sports field. I pursued athletics because I was competitive and enjoyed the camaraderie. Also, I am vain, so I liked how exercise made me look.

I joke that where I came from—the son of a single mother who fed her kids with food stamps and from a family where only some people go to college—I should be managing a rental car agency. As I climbed the academic mountain, especially, my modest beginnings made every small achievement feel monumental and fueled my motivation to strive for greater achievements. Success was exhilarating and set up a fly wheel for further opportunities.

My focus began to shift in my forties as I discovered the joys of creation. I started to identify as a "creative" person and began to shape my schedule to support that endeavor. Waking early to spend hours writing in coffee shops, I found my work increasingly flow-worthy. I enjoyed solving puzzles, whether crafting esoteric sentences or figuring out what makes things funny. The creative work benefited my career and leads to moments where time melts away.

With time, achievements via academia and athletics didn't lose their allure, but rather their importance as I stumbled into the Solo movement. I found my ambitions were not solely tethered to professional accolades or wins on the sports field. I am now doing my most meaningful work. I am obsessed with helping my single sisters and brothers.

Perhaps you are happy with how you are flourishing. I don't see Henry Rollins making big changes to the way he lives, but perhaps you are ready to start a new chapter. With a foundation in place, you get to experiment, but I hope you'll soon be catching wind via purpose, engagement, or positive emotion (or some combination thereof).

## PURPOSE

Lisa Lampanelli has undergone a remarkable transformation. She began her stand-up comedy career in the 1990s, quickly becoming known for her edgy, self-deprecating comedy. Imagine Lampanelli at the height of her comedy career: bold, brazen, and hurling razor-sharp insults with unapologetic flair. The stage was her battleground, and wit, her weapon. Lampanelli became a regular on *Comedy Central Roasts*, excoriating celebrities such as David Hasselhoff, Pamela Anderson, and Flava Flav. She earned the title of "The Queen of Mean."

Picture a starkly different scene: Lampanelli, calm and empathetic, standing in front of an audience not to mock, but to motivate; not to ridicule, but to inspire. She grew weary of hurting people with her words. She traded her barbs for a mantle of advocacy, supporting mental health, body positivity, and self-improvement. Her remarkable metamorphosis began with that realization in 2018. By confronting and addressing her personal challenges, she transformed them into powerful stories of growth and redemption. A deeper purpose. She's reigned over a kingdom of laughs; now she's building a legacy of meaning. The "Queen of Mean" has evolved into the "Queen of Meaning."

A purposeful life helps serve as a psychological shield of sorts: Depression and anxiety appear less daunting to those who have a strong sense of purpose. Finding purpose often helps facilitate forging and maintaining stronger bonds. That has been the case for me. The Solo project has exposed me to new, wonderful people who have become friends, and the project has fostered a community of singles who once felt isolated. Join us!

## Meaning

A meaningful life is a life of purpose that benefits others by doing something challenging that is bigger than yourself. A journey that transcends personal needs could involve dedicating time to a humanitarian cause or nonprofit, such as the Peace Corps. Meaningful living might also manifest in a quest to solve significant problems through scientific research, such as aiming to eradicate disease. Perhaps it takes the form of nurturing potential in others through teaching, coaching, or mentoring. You could find purpose in providing aid in disaster-hit regions, advocating for social policies promoting equity, or inspiring others through creating art, literature, or music. For others, organizing community events to promote unity, taking care of an elderly parent, or starting a family are meaningful pursuits.

## Achievement

A life of achievement is a life of purpose that benefits the self by doing something challenging that is bigger than yourself. Achievement sometimes gets a bad rap, often seen as selfish—especially looking at folks who seek to make money for its own sake ("Greed is good") or to conquer the world (literally). Yet in lots of cases, doing something bigger than yourself for yourself is a great way to flourish through personal or professional growth.

Achievement centers on tackling personal challenges. It could entail mastering a complex subject or skill, like coding or a new language, or pushing physical boundaries by training for a marathon or an ultra-marathon. This journey might involve academic advancement through acquiring a higher degree or professional certification. Achievements can also be in the realm of arts and culture. Imagine the great challenge of becoming a stand-up comedian. Entrepreneurial pursuits such as starting and growing a business fall within this sphere, as do adventure-based goals like mountain climbing. Participating in competitions, completing ambitious projects like building a house, or becoming a polymath are also achievement-oriented endeavors.

Achievement is a path for many people to strive for a better existence, have more purpose in their day-to-day. The journey toward achievement is frequently marked by personal growth and development. Striving for success involves acquiring new skills, overcoming challenges, and moving beyond comfort zones. This process often leads to an improved sense of self-efficacy and self-esteem.

Let's look at a real-life example of how someone turned challenges into remarkable achievements. James Warner, an IT consultant and proud Solo in Denver, is the youngest of seven children. His family navigated homelessness, food insecurity, violence, alcoholism, and drug addiction. In his words, "It took most of my twenties and thirties, but I was able to cobble a path upward and out of poverty."

For Warner's fortieth birthday, he undertook two significant challenges related to his beauty and brains. He set out on a one-year endeavor to perform stand-up comedy and compete in a bodybuilding competition (not on the same night). His foray into bodybuilding was successful, placing fifth in the open heavy weights division. His brief comedy career was similarly successful; he won an amateur showcase and earned a paid spot in the headlining show the following week. The Ancient Greeks would be proud.

Warner, a fun, self-deprecating character, views his life as a scrapbook: "I want to pack as many cool experiences in as I can before I take my final bow." If Warner was riding the relationship escalator, I suspect he would have failed to add comedy *and* bodybuilding to his scrapbook. Just imagine as he heads out to the gym to pump iron or to a late-night open mic to workshop some jokes, his husband whines, "Honey, are you going out, again?"[1]

Singles are trailblazers. Singles have the flexibility and mobility that make them a formidable force for innovation. They are not as encumbered by the opportunity costs that married people often face, granting them the freedom to contribute significantly if they so desire. Entrepreneurs, particularly single ones, can build businesses that make people's lives better. People engaged in major endeavors like eradicating disease—or even those who bring joy through books, poetry, and music—need the freedom to work long hours, as the fruits of their labor are tremendously beneficial.

The pursuit of achievement also has noteworthy social implications. Achievements often necessitate teamwork and collaboration, leading to the development of improved social skills and relationships. The recognition and celebration of accomplishments by others can foster increased social support and a deepened sense of community.

Pay attention to what naturally piques your interest. What are the topics that energize you when you talk about them? Where do you observe a gap that you feel compelled to fill? Often, it's in these spaces that purpose resides.

Purpose offers a reason to skip the snooze button, but a life lived in pursuit of purpose is akin to seeking the golden fleece—a noble quest, but one that brings the threat of dragons:

- **Imbalance.** Having it all—work, family, social life, personal interests—is difficult. Though, if you're single, you might have more wiggle room in that department.

- **Expectations.** Beware the shadows of uncertainty and the anxiety associated with the prospect of both success and the fear of failure. Despite doing everything "right," one might still fall short of a goal. This dragon also feeds on the disappointment that comes from failure. Striving for achievement often necessitates external validation, thus putting your happiness in the hands of others. Ask the author who judges the success of a book based on sales.

- **Sacrifice.** There are costs and opportunity costs associated with purposeful pursuits. Pursing achievement or meaning often involves trading immediate pleasures for longer-term fulfillment. Raising a child, for instance, can bestow immeasurable fulfillment, but it often comes with stress, anxiety, and loss of sleep. Achievement often demands prolonged periods of work and attention. If success were effortless, everyone would do it. Thus, this dragon's flames can create burnout.

## ENGAGEMENT

Sisyphus, the mythical Greek trickster, broke divine rules and was punished by the gods. His task was to roll a colossal boulder up a hill. His punishment was intended to be a futile, never-ending task. Every time Sisyphus nears the summit, the boulder slips from his grasp and rolls back down, rendering his labor seemingly utterly pointless. He begins this task again, laboring for eternity. But what if the gods' punishment was misguided? What if Sisyphus was happy?

Albert Camus was obsessed with how to find freedom in a world that he saw as largely devoid of meaning. Born in 1913 in Algeria, Camus witnessed the horrors of war and human suffering. The violent struggle for independence in his homeland, Algeria, heightened his disillusionment. The hardship of growing up in poverty, the early loss of his father, and his own battle with tuberculosis compounded his view of life's harshness and arbitrariness.

In his unique brand of optimism, Camus saw Sisyphus's act not as a futile exercise but as a way to live remarkably. It is not the outcome that matters, but the process where people can seek engagement, finding satisfaction in seemingly routine activities, by being fully present and creating challenge.

Camus illustrates his perspective in his essay *The Myth of Sisyphus*. Instead of a focus on the outcome—reaching the peak—engagement is about the challenge of pursuing the peak. There is freedom in the striving and strain. Camus suggests there is opportunity within the journey. Camus ends the essay with the famous line "One must imagine Sisyphus happy," solidifying his argument that engagement is an act of living, creating, and rebelling against unjust gods.

Solos that can see opportunities in seemingly redundant tasks offer a chance for a perspective shift. It is through engagement that one can find satisfaction in the repetitive nature of certain tasks. This can be mirrored in daily life by finding engagement in activities we often take for granted. Now, what Sisyphean tasks in your life hold the potential for engagement? What steps could you take to be like Sisyphus, finding happiness and engagement in the journey, rather than the destination?

Flow is a psychological term that describes a state of complete immersion in an activity. Time seems to disappear and one's sense of self blends into the action at hand. Flow occurs when a person becomes so absorbed in a task that all else seems to fade away. This concept was formulated by the psychologist Mihaly Csikszentmihalyi, who once noted, "The best moments in our lives are not the passive, receptive, relaxing times. . . . The best moments usually occur if a person's body or mind is stretched to its limits in a voluntary effort to accomplish something difficult and worthwhile."

Engagement in life can take many forms. Perhaps you're drawn to writing, delving into narratives or nonfiction topics. Learning a new language with its rich complexities captivates.

Others enjoy painting, where colors, forms, and textures create an immersive experience. Coding presents an avenue for problem-solving, while athletics or exercise merge physical exertion with focus, inducing a state of flow. Entrepreneurship requires deep focus from conception to execution, while data analysis can fully engage the mind. Mastering a musical instrument or composing music, gardening, or experimenting with culinary techniques can also lead to this immersive experience.

A 2022 study by Chang and colleagues in the journal *Leisure Sciences* reveals the therapeutic potential of engaging in complex yet engaging activities, known to induce a state of flow, as a way to mitigate loneliness. The study offers a tangible and, more importantly, practicable solution to loneliness—immersing oneself in stimulating pursuits that facilitate a state of flow. This active involvement mirrors athletes being "in the zone" or artists lost in their craft.

I like to ask my friends and podcast listeners, "Are you living on your edge?" A key aspect of flow is balancing skill and challenge. An activity that is too easy is boring, while one that is too challenging creates anxiety. Flow is achieved when the challenge at hand matches the skill level (figure 7). It's why the best athletes and world-class musicians thrive on the biggest stages. Flow is not restricted to grandiose achievements; it permeates everyday life. For instance, when engrossed in a captivating book, the world around you might dissolve away. Or perhaps when solving a complex puzzle, your focus sharpens and time seems to warp. Even in hobbies like gardening, there's a peace and focus that comes with planting.

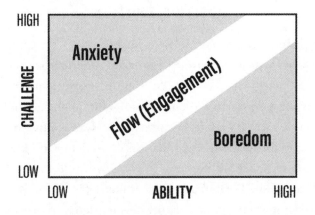

**FIGURE 7:** Mihaly Csikszentmihalyi's Flow Model shows the association between the ability level (x-axis) of an individual and the challenge of a task (y-axis). Matching ability and challenge results in a state of flow (Csikszentmihalyi, 1990).

Flow involves a merging of action and awareness. Flow states may be associated with a goal-oriented task, but also marked by a desire to accomplish something within the task. It involves micro-goals and immediate feedback, which contributes to the feeling of making progress even on small tasks, such as word choice for a writer or a single brushstroke for a painter.

I have a saying, "Create more than you consume." In the pursuit of personal growth and flow, I present a bold proposition: Aspire to be a creator. Few people choose to tread the path of creation, which can encompass a wide array of flow-worthy activities. Fair warning. I have another saying for those who put their creations into the world: So difficult to create, yet so easy to criticize.

## POSITIVE EMOTION

Some people work to live. I live to work.

My stereotypical life as an overworked American started with survival. Facing financial and housing insecurity from a young age, my solution was to work my way out of it. That, coupled with the naïve idea that I could become a professor, led me to throw myself into the challenging endeavors of academia. If I knew the base rate of academic success, I probably would have taken a government job. Fortunately, the bet paid off.

Reflecting on my good fortune and tendency to overwork, a friend and collaborator Caleb Warren asked me, "What will play look like to you in the next three to five months? Three to five years?" I had no idea how to answer that question. I work every day. I keep a tight schedule. I don't vacation. Yes, I am flourishing through the Solo project, writing, podcasting, speaking, teaching, and conducting academic research. However, what is the use of all the sacrifices—the Saturday nights in my office—if I don't leverage my success to enjoy a life that is more than half over?

A remarkable life does not need to be a happy life. Though, a happy life is typically a remarkable life. The Greek philosopher Aristotle argued that "*eudaimonia,*" which often translates as "happiness," but a more accurate translation would be "flourishing" or "living well," is the highest good to which all human activities should aim. The "hedonic" school of thought, represented by philosophers like Epicurus, on the other hand, is centered on the pursuit of pleasure and the avoidance of pain as the primary drivers of happiness. Epicurus emphasized the simple pleasures of life, such as friendship, intellectual conversations, and modest living. In modern context, this could translate to finding joy in social gatherings, indulging in hobbies, or taking vacations to recharge.

The experience of positive emotions (and removal of negative emotions) brings numerous benefits, from bolstering health to enhancing creativity and an ability to cope with stress. The range of positive emotions within a day is vast, with each emotion having unique characteristics and effects. Sensory pleasures, such as laughter from a comedy, the thrill of an adventure, the delight of tasty cuisine, and the euphoria of music and dance, stimulate an array of positive emotional responses. These experiences allow us to engage with our environment, creating memorable moments that bring joy and satisfaction. Emotional pleasures like delight, joy, curiosity, imagination, fun, and love are central to our emotional repertoire.

Emotions are a source of information; they teach us how to behave in the future. Biologically, some emotions stem from our evolutionary past. For instance, the pleasure derived from play fighting and tickling is the basis for comedy. Physical touch and intimacy are also rooted in our biology, promoting a sense of connection and belonging, which are essential for our survival. Cultural influences also significantly shape our emotional experiences. The awe experienced during a performance or the joy of a team's victory are examples of how cultural and subjective contexts can affect our emotions. Specific rituals and customs, like celebrating birthdays and holidays, can evoke feelings of happiness and togetherness. Perhaps even gender reveal parties.

## Sex and Taste
It is important to recognize the importance of a healthy and satisfying sex life and address the cultural and social barriers

that hinder it. More important, for those who value sex, it is essential to see sex not as an indulgence, but as an excellent source of positive emotion.

According to the "the rules," people who partner up get to have sex. Singles don't unless it is a precursor to a "serious" relationship. Access to sex and intimacy is a major motivator to ride the escalator, as evidenced by a 2022 study by Park and MacDonald that reveals singles who are satisfied with their sex life expressed lower desire for a relationship partner.

A prohibition of sex before marriage comes from lots of places, but one historical figure we can attribute some of the blame to is England's Queen Victoria, who screwed us by making it harder to screw. The sexual repression that emerged during the Victorian era still affects Western culture today. Victoria's reign, with its strict moral codes and societal norms, profoundly influenced attitudes toward sex, casting it as necessary for procreation, rather than as an enjoyable aspect of human life.

The regulation of sex during this time was also, in part, about regulating women. The Victorian era's repression laid the groundwork for a backlash, the sexual revolution of the 1960s. The revolution saw a societal shift, challenging traditional norms around sexuality and advocating for sexual liberation. Yet, as history has shown us, progress and regression often go hand in hand.

It's acceptable not to have sex if one doesn't want to, but it's not acceptable for others to impose their opinions on someone's personal choice. Sex is a powerful stress reliever and contributes to a good night's sleep (in other words, flourishing also helps your foundation). Sex helps people bond. Generally speaking, sex is good for people, and for those who want it, not having enough of it negatively affects health and happiness.

Singles can have greater sexual variety and novelty if they want it. However, data from the General Social Survey indicates that the number of people having sex at least once a week has been dropping, particularly among young people. About 23 percent of women and 30 percent of men under thirty reported no sexual activity in the past year.

The decline in sexual activity is a complex topic, and while behavioral scientists are trying to figure this out, there is not yet consensus. Though you might guess a major culprit: your (damn) phone. Moreover, many people prioritize careers and education, and the demanding nature of modern work and academic life leaves little room for romantic and sexual relationships. Moreover, the rise in mental health issues, such as anxiety and depression, can notably dampen sexual desire and satisfaction (as do the drugs that treat them). Fear of sexually transmitted infections also plays a role, thus it is up to the individual to decide how to navigate those risks with testing, safe sex, and communication.

Another case for flourishing via positive emotion is to develop a taste for the good things in life. Taste is commonly defined as a personal preference, particularly toward aesthetics in art, design, and experiences. Good taste is a learned skill, cultivated through education, exposure, and experience. The enjoyment of aesthetic experiences such as music, art, clothing, food, and decor is influenced by the ease of processing and repeated exposure.

This echoes the French approach to pleasure—emphasizing quality over quantity, and guilt-free enjoyment of life's simple pleasures. Becoming more "French" in your pursuit of pleasure is to immerse yourself in the process of appreciation and refinement. Slow down, savor an experience whether it's sipping a cappuccino, enjoying a symphony, or picking the perfect baguette (*and* give up the guilt). The French know this secret well: To truly live is to taste life fully, with discernment, elegance, and an appetite for joie de vivre. For a crash course, I recommend watching *Ratatouille*.

In conclusion, cultivating positive emotions involves a delicate balance and mindfulness. Know yourself, embrace community, savor experiences, and, most important, allow yourself to live a life rich with both variety and depth.

As we approach the end of this book, it's time to recognize the progress you, the reader, have made. Earlier, we discussed how the negative stereotypes around singles can contribute to their own negative perception of singlehood. However, now, as you transition to a full-fledged Solo, I hope you are beginning to see how you can live remarkably. To do so requires knowing yourself.

And a little alone time will help that endeavor.

## SOLO LOVE LETTER

**Steve, Retired Tech Sales Guy, Raleigh, North Carolina, USA**

**A day in my solo life:**

**Morning:**

- Wake up at 3:00 a.m.
- Feed the dogs.
- Walk with dog for forty-five minutes, enjoying the silent darkness.
- Three hours of gymnastics and yoga.
- Swim for an hour.
- Shopping/library/vet as needed.

- Eat breakfast.
- Walk dog on nature trails.

**Afternoon:**

- Tackle current DIY project.
- Do chores—cleaning, vacuuming, lawn mowing, laundry, batch cook food.
- Hobbies—Write blog posts, paint, draw, drum.
- Siesta—thirty-minute afternoon nap, if tired.

**Evening:**

- Casual forty-five-minute stroll with both dogs. Socialize with neighbors and other walkers.
- Catch up with Mom and friends by phone.
- Feed dogs.
- Eat dinner.
- Reading, internet browsing, participate in forums, research DIY projects, watch dog rescue videos and stream shows.
- Fall asleep before 8:00 p.m.

I met my future wife when I was twenty-one. She was eighteen years older, recently separated, and had two kids (ages five and ten). I moved in within weeks, and we were together for twenty-nine years. In 2018, she was diagnosed with lung cancer and died eight months later. There are times when being Solo can be challenging. I miss my wife. I have to rely on friends and neighbors more now. I used to miss having someone to talk to; now I blog more and enjoy conversations with casual acquaintances. I tried online dating, but it was not enjoyable. I have not yet met anyone IRL and have little interest in pursuing a relationship.

I don't suffer from many of the societal challenges, anxiety, expectations, or slights that other Solos often mention. I suspect it's because I am a loner, a man, highly self-confident, and don't care what other people think about me. Plus, being a widower is a built-in social shield.

I am often alone but almost never lonely. For me, being Solo is remarkable. I will never go back to living with someone or riding the escalator. I did that already. It was wonderful in its own way but that chapter of my life is closed.

## SOLO LOVE LETTER

### Suzette, Project Manager and Organizer, Alexandria, Virginia, USA

When I was thirty-two, I had a terrible evening at a wedding. I was too embarrassed to attend by myself. I believed that attending a wedding alone was a sign of my undesirability, so I asked my friend Don to go with me. But Don was a deadweight more than a party starter. We sat together at a table feeling bored. I wanted to dance with my friends, but I didn't want to leave Don alone. It wasn't fun—and we left early. I threw myself on my bed that night declaring: "I hate weddings!"

I started wondering what it would be like to be more confident in my singleness. So, I began to do more things by myself. I was nervous at first. The first movie I attended alone, I wondered if people would think I was weird or if I would feel lonely. Ultimately, it was great! I got to choose my movie, my seat, and my snack.

The first time I had lunch by myself, I was nervous, too. But I sat outside in the sun and smiled at the people passing on the street.

They smiled back and were not concerned at all that I was eating alone, so I relaxed.

When I went to a museum by myself, I wandered through the paintings at my own pace. I chatted with strangers and made new friends. They liked me. And I liked me.

My relationship circles expanded. Marriage was no longer a requirement for my happiness. My friends embraced my single life—and so did I.

I was recently invited to another wedding. I paused over the RSVP card before deciding I would go alone. It was wonderful. I sat at a table with my friends and danced all night. When I came home and threw myself onto my bed, I went peacefully to sleep. I don't know when my next wedding invitation will arrive, but I know I will RSVP for one with pleasure.

# THIRTEEN

# The Case for Solitude

Virginia Woolf was born into a prominent literary family in London in 1882. Her father, Sir Leslie Stephen, was a renowned author and editor, and her mother, Julia Jackson, was a well-known artist. Growing up in such an intellectually and artistically stimulating environment had a profound impact on her creativity. Woolf was constantly questioning the rules.

In 1929, she penned the famous book *A Room of One's Own*, which explored why female writers were neither as plentiful nor as successful as male writers. Woolf concluded women had little opportunity for creative expression because they had neither time nor space for solitude. They were too preoccupied with caregiving. She advocated that women needed the financial means to support themselves so that they didn't have to rely on men for their livelihood. They also needed space and time to think and write without distraction.

Women needed a room of their own.

Just nine years later, Marjorie Hillis, a successful editor and writer for *Vogue* magazine, authored *Live Alone and Like It: A Guide for the Extra Woman*. The guide was written for single women on how to enjoy and make the most of their independence.

Ultimately a book about parenting yourself, it offered guidance from decorating and entertaining to finances and solo travel. The book was a cultural revelation, selling more than five hundred thousand copies. President Franklin D. Roosevelt was spotted reading a copy.

The "extra woman" was a term used in the 1920s and 1930s to refer to single, independent women who bucked traditional gender roles, especially marriage and family. These spinsters were considered "extra" because they did not fit into the societal norm of the time. Hillis preferred the term "Live Aloners" because it reflects a positive choice to spend time in solitude.

Recognizing and appreciating the opportunities of solitude is a crucial step for the aspiring Solo. Yes, spending time alone comes with its challenges—just like singlehood—but it also harbors incredible potential. Alone time provides opportunities for rest and recovery, fosters self-reflection, encourages spiritual pursuits, and ignites creativity. Perhaps most importantly, it offers Solos a remarkable chance to spend quality time with the most significant person in their lives: themselves.

Scholars and laypeople assert that humans are social creatures, but being social doesn't demand constant socialization. Balancing solitude and connection is critical. Few people are legitimate lone wolves, just as no one wants to be at an endless rave.

While social scientists have been preoccupied with the very real issue of loneliness, only a few have looked at the opposite phenomenon, called *aloneliness*, the stressful experience of having too little solitude. While humans are social creatures and most people need to be around others at least some of the time, being constantly around people can be too much. According to a Hamilton Project survey in 2020, 79 percent of married mothers felt that they did not have enough time to themselves, whereas single women were much less likely to report such an experience.

I have an old friend from college, Tony, who has a wife and three or four kids. Just kidding. It's three. I am sure of it.

Tony is a world-class father, but being a parent is difficult. When his kids were young, Tony had a unique way of enjoying solitude amidst his hectic life. He had this thing—he was probably the only person at the airport who was stoked when his plane was delayed. While the rest of the airport's population goes into meltdown mode, dialing customer service or tweeting their fury, there's Tony with a twinkle in his eye. He heads to the airport bookstore and picks out a book and finds a quiet place to read and stave off aloneliness.

Just like Goldilocks in the classic fairy tale, who sought porridge that was neither too hot nor too cold but just right, finding the right balance between socialization and solitude is key. Tony recognized this "Goldilocks solution" to social connections. Having this time alone allowed him to decompress, reflect, and learn something new.

In contrast to Tony, singles often have more control over their time. They can choose when to socialize and when to enjoy solitude. This balance is achieved with intention, as they consciously make time for reflection and personal growth. Like Tony, singles find their own "Goldilocks solution," tailored to their lifestyle, through a blend of social connections and solitude.

Concerns about loneliness often overshadow the numerous benefits that solitude offers, especially when it is used constructively. It's not just the solitude that matters. It matters what you do with it.

Much has been made of research in the journal *Science* that shows people's preference for a mild electric shock over sitting in a room alone for fifteen minutes. Interpretations of the study, however, unfairly characterize solitude. If you start a new meditation program, you are not asked to sit quietly with your thoughts for fifteen minutes. You have to work up to that. The research was designed to create boredom, and boredom is aversive. I like being alone, but not with nothing to do. If given a choice between sitting idly with nothing to do and a quick shock to pass the time, why not? But if you give me paper and pencil or a book to read? Can I have an extra thirty minutes? And please close the door on your way out and take your shocking machine with you!

Solitude has many benefits if you use it wisely. While solitude is good for teenagers' development, time spent on social media is not.

## CREATIVITY

I am no recluse, but I appreciate the appeal of the lone wolf, who stands outside of society's status hierarchy. When I was young, I entertained the possibility of becoming a university president. A lofty goal, considering my humble state school education. In hindsight, such a prestigious position would have brought me misery, being chained to a calendar filled with meetings under fluorescent lights. Today, I'd much rather spend my time sitting in a cozy café, sipping cappuccinos, immersed in creative work.

I aspire to create more than I consume. Solitude benefits that creation process, as demonstrated by studies. For instance, research by Gregory Feist reveals that people who embrace solitude are more likely to engage in creative activities. Additionally, research by Ruth shows a positive association between time spent in solitude and the generation of original ideas.

Research indicates that people who spend time in solitude tend to participate in "constructive internal reflection," which aids in generating creative concepts. The study also revealed that introverted people tend to benefit more from solitude in this way than extroverted people. No surprise there.

The benefits of solitude to creative pursuits are striking. People who choose to live alone or intentionally carve out time for solitude within conventional relationships, are overrepresented among creative types, especially in literature. Fenton Johnson, in his book *At the Center of All Beauty: Solitude and the Creative Life,* profiles iconic solitaires such as Walt Whitman, Nina Simone, Emily Dickinson, and Henry David Thoreau. In his book *Daily Rituals,* Mason Curry reveals how great minds, from Voltaire to Einstein to Joan Didion, typically created alone.

A notable exception was Jane Austen, who had to write in the living room of her parents' house and hide her notes when guests arrived. While many iconic creatives relished in their solitude, Jane Austen's genius flourished despite her crowded environment—though we can only dream of what she might have accomplished in the tranquil sanctity of a room of her own.

## REST, RECOVERY, AND REFLECTION

I celebrate solitude as an opportunity to rest, recover, and reflect. Anyone who takes a break after a romantic breakup knows the value of time spent alone.

Ever catch yourself saying, "I need to be alone," when you are upset? Imagine being in prison where you can't get any alone time. Prisoners will lie in bed and turn their face to the wall and say "I'm in my feelings" to anyone who comes by—and it is understood that you leave the person alone.

Research confirms what your body intuitively knows. A study published in the *Journal of Research in Personality* in 2014, by Nguyen, Ryan, and Deci, found that spending time alone can mitigate negative emotions. Turns out people experience less intense emotions when they're alone compared to when they're with others, which the authors suggest is due to the absence of social feedback when alone.

In the fast-paced world we live in, finding time for rest and recovery can be a challenge. Research supports the idea that being alone can be helpful for recovering from stress and trauma. For example, a study published in the journal *Health Psychology* in 2015 by Thoma and colleagues reveals that solitude can facilitate lower stress levels and promote psychological recovery. Being alone provides a safe space for people to process their emotions and experiences without external distractions or pressures.

I have lived alone most of my adulthood while also keeping a vigorous social calendar. Lately, I have been obsessed by creative work—writing, reading, and podcasting. Rather than keeping an exhausting social calendar or traveling on a plane, I have been spending time alone to travel in my mind. If you're looking for a truly restorative experience, time alone in nature is particularly beneficial for both mental and physical health.

Solitude also facilitates reflection—spiritual or otherwise.

Research reveals that solitude can help people gain a greater sense of purpose and meaning in life. For instance, a 2003 study by Long and Averill in *Psychological Bulletin* shows solitude can facilitate self-discovery and personal growth by allowing individuals to engage deeply with their thoughts and emotions. This introspective process in solitude can lead to a clearer understanding of one's values and priorities. Another 2018 study by Nguyen and colleagues in *Personality and Social Psychology Bulletin* revealed that spending time alone can foster a sense of autonomy and independence, which contributes to a person's sense of self-worth.

Throughout history, many religious and spiritual traditions also recognize the value of solitude for reflection and spiritual growth. Jesus spent forty days alone in the desert. (And his reward? Being tempted by Satan.) Monastic traditions across Christian, Buddhist, and Hindu cultures incorporate periods of solitude and silence for contemplation and prayer. For instance, Buddhist monks often go on Vipassana retreats, which involve meditating in silence for extended periods, while Native American tribes have long practiced vision quests, where tribesmen would go into the wilderness alone to gain spiritual insights and guidance. The prophet Muhammad allegedly received his first revelation during a period of reflection in the cave of Hira.

Those happy monks with all that solitude and their super happy brains seem to be on to something.

## MAXIMIZING EXPERIENCES

"Ignore the banalities and the mundane things seen on television or read in newspapers. To be free and alone in the maze of the city, the flâneur craves of revelation that might change his or her life." So says Federico Castigliano in his book *Flâneur: The Art of Wandering the Streets of Paris*. Academic, author, and happy Solo, Federico taught me about flâneuring—the act of wandering aimlessly through a city and taking in the sights, sounds, and smells of a cityscape with no particular destination in mind.

The concept of flâneuring emerged in late-nineteenth-century Parisian culture, referring to a person of means who would dress up and stroll around the city with no particular goal in mind. Through their wanderings, flâneurs could explore the city and see it from a unique perspective, detached from the hustle and bustle of everyday life.

Federico contends that Paris is the ideal city for flâneuring, due to its wide boulevards, stunning architecture, plentiful parks, and excellent people-watching opportunities. In any case, when it comes to flâneuring, Federico suggests it's best undertaken solo. The reason? It allows you to fully immerse yourself in the experience without the need for compromise or coordination. The concept of flâneuring recognizes that sometimes people add value to an experience, but other times they distract. Distractions might arise because an activity partner is not the best company, or simply because of incompatibility. Research that examines solo versus shared experiences in the *Journal of Marketing Research* by Wu and colleagues in 2021 finds that when people need to make joint decisions, they tend to focus on aligning their preferences. This alignment often involves making trade-offs about what to do or what to buy, which can lead to a less optimal outcome for both parties compared to their initial singular desires. Think about a compromise movie.

Going out alone avoids the need to cooperate with others. Solo moviegoers choose the movie they want, choose the start time they want, and pick the seat they want. (They also feel less guilty about eating an entire bag of popcorn.)

## Alone, Not at Home

Despite the benefits of solitude, people remain reluctant to do things alone. Much of the reluctance is caused by the belief that people will perceive them as sad and lonely. These feelings are exacerbated by the "spotlight effect," where people suspect everyone will notice that stain on their shirt when few notice in reality (and when they do, the observer couldn't care less).

In Japan, these misguided intuitions lead people to hire the "do-nothing guy," Shoji Morimoto, a man who gets paid just to be a warm body. Some people feel such societal pressure to avoid doing things alone that they're willing to pay Shoji for company: walking a client to a job interview, attending a book launch, or simply sharing a cup of coffee. As he once said in an interview: "I'm not a friend or an acquaintance. I'm free of the bothersome things that accompany relationships but can ease people's sense of loneliness."

If you are wondering, Morimoto is married.

I was curious what activities people do alone. Some would seem obvious, like shopping. Others less so. Concerts? Comedy shows? Hunting? To answer that question, I surveyed single and married Americans, asking them about their lone participation in twenty-five public activities. Most activities were pleasurable (e.g., concerts, movies), others were practical (e.g., shopping), and a few were set in the outdoors (hiking, fishing).

Respondents were asked if they participated in the activity, and if so, did they do it alone ("Yes, often," "Yes, rarely," or "Not at all"). Only respondents who said they participated in the activity were included in the analyses.

First, there is a huge range in responses from the highest "alone" activity (clothes shopping, with over 95 percent for both groups) to the lowest (skiing, 18.5 percent for single vs. 9.5 percent for married respondents). Results are reported in table 2.

Singles are much more likely to do things alone in public than their married counterparts (56 percent vs. 39 percent, respectively). The difference pattern held for all of the twenty-five activities. For differences between married and single, the smallest was shopping for clothes. The biggest difference was going to the movies (58 percent for single vs. 25 percent for married respondents). Interestingly, seven out the ten largest differences were related to retail experiences, such as concerts and dining (see table 3).

The data from the survey made me simultaneously happy and sad. First, I was happy to see so many singles going out in the world and living life—going to concerts, visiting museums, hiking, and even hunting. (The nice thing about hunting alone is that it's harder to be shot accidentally.) These singles are not waiting around for someone to complete them and give them an excuse to live life.

I also felt bad for married people who are likely skipping activities that they want to do alone or are getting dragged along to events that they don't really want to do.

Research by Hamilton and Ratner published in 2015 in the *Journal of Consumer Research* examined biases that keep people from doing things alone in public. I spoke to Hamilton about the finding and she noted how consistent the bias is across cultures:

> When we compared activity preferences among consumers currently living in China, those currently living in India, and those currently living in the United States, we found that all three groups were significantly less interested in seeing a movie at a theater alone than in seeing the same movie at a theater with two or more friends. Although they would be seeing the very same movie, they anticipated enjoying it less when alone than with friends.

| ACTIVITY ALONE | SINGLES | MARRIED | DIFFERENCE |
|---|---|---|---|
| Shop for Clothes | 96% | 95% | 1% |
| Walk | 95% | 87% | 8% |
| Shop for Groceries | 94% | 88% | 5% |
| Run | 83% | 75% | 8% |
| Coffee Shop | 80% | 67% | 13% |
| Domestic Travel | 78% | 65% | 14% |
| Bike | 74% | 53% | 21% |
| Hike | 65% | 41% | 24% |
| Casual Dining | 64% | 41% | 23% |
| Museum | 58% | 31% | 27% |
| Movies | 58% | 25% | 33% |
| Road Trips | 57% | 42% | 15% |
| Fishing or Hunting | 53% | 30% | 23% |
| International Travel | 52% | 41% | 11% |
| Theater | 51% | 21% | 30% |
| Bars | 49% | 20% | 29% |
| Mountain Biking | 48% | 35% | 13% |
| Dinner Party | 47% | 26% | 21% |
| Concert | 42% | 16% | 26% |
| Wedding | 38% | 22% | 16% |
| Fine Dining | 34% | 11% | 23% |
| Sporting Event | 28% | 22% | 6% |
| Dance Club | 27% | 10% | 17% |
| Comedy Show | 22% | 11% | 11% |
| Skiing | 19% | 10% | 9% |

**TABLE 2:** Data from Single Insights: The Science of Solos (2022). Frequency of doing activities alone between single and married Americans (N = 254). The table displays twenty-five public activities and the percentage of respondents who participate in these activities alone. Data ranges from the most common to least common activities for singles. Differences in frequency is always greater for single respondents.

| ACTIVITY ALONE | SINGLES | MARRIED | DIFFERENCE |
|---|---|---|---|
| Movie | 58% | 25% | 33% |
| Theatre | 51% | 21% | 30% |
| Bar | 49% | 20% | 29% |
| Museum | 58% | 31% | 27% |
| Concert | 42% | 16% | 26% |
| Hiking | 65% | 41% | 24% |
| Casual Dining | 64% | 41% | 23% |
| Fishing/Hunting | 53% | 30% | 23% |
| Fine Dining | 34% | 11% | 23% |
| Dinner Party | 47% | 26% | 21% |

**TABLE 3:** The largest differences in doing things alone in public between single and married people. Data from Single Insights: The Science of Solos (2022).

To debunk that belief, the researchers conducted a study on the University of Maryland campus, where some people went to an art gallery alone and others went with another person. Though the respondents who went alone predicted they'd have a less favorable experience, they ended up enjoying it just as much as if they were with another person.

## SOLITUDE: A WAY TO LOVE YOURSELF

Greta Garbo quipped, "I never said, 'I want to be alone.' I only said, 'I want to be left alone.' There is a difference." Having quality alone time allows you to check in with yourself and know yourself. This is important for anyone, whether single or in a relationship, but single people have the advantage of having much more opportunity for solitude. Moreover, the pillars of Soloness—being wholehearted, self-sufficient, and an unconventional thinker—are integral to embracing solitude and harnessing its benefits, especially if you eventually partner up.

- **Feeling Complete:** Being a whole person entails finding peace within, especially when alone. Solos don't need to find someone else for companionship; one's own company is enough.
- **Independence and Self-Reliance:** These are critical when seeking a Goldilocks balance between connection and alone time. Being self-sufficient means you can be more discerning in choosing when to seek the company of others and when to relish your own company.
- **Being an Unconventional Thinker:** Recognizing the unwritten rules dictating what you should do with others and what you can do alone is liberating. With this understanding, you can feel comfortable and confident being alone, without concern for what others *might think.*

If you are interested in spending more time alone with yourself, I suggest starting small by experimenting with intentional solitude. You could begin with the first activity on the list in table 2 and work your way down until you find something you haven't tried alone yet. Perhaps you start modestly in a dark movie theater, then level up by eating out at a hotel bar, and eventually venture into solo fine dining. For the ultimate challenge, grab a reservation on Valentine's Day at a couple-focused restaurant (and read this book) or go out dancing alone (as my friend Darwyn does). If that doesn't whet your appetite, try going to a comedy show. (Note: Comedians don't pick on the single person in the crowd. Lone wolves themselves, comedians prefer to make fun of the couples. Plus the host won't seat you in the front anyway.)

Walking is another excellent opportunity to experiment with solitude. Revive the lost art of flâneuring. Like the original flâneurs, dress up a little to enhance your confidence. You can ease into this by heading out with a friend and agreeing to split up for a while before meeting again at a designated time. If safety is a concern, schedule check-ins or use a tracking app so someone can keep tabs on you.

Finally, lean into the activities you naturally enjoy doing alone. Are you going to the gym by yourself? Do you frequent a local coffee shop with friendly baristas where you like to journal or read? Do you find yourself savoring a quiet Friday night to cook or paint? Be intentional about this time; turn off your (damn) phone and immerse yourself in the activity.

The key is to find a balance between connection and solitude that feels just right. And who knows? Maybe the next time you're stuck at the airport, you'll take a page out of Tony's book (pun intended) and dive into a good read.

# WHAT ARE YOU WAITING FOR?

**M**arie Edwards and Eleanor Hoover coauthored a book that documents the challenge of being single, aptly titled *The Challenge of Being Single*. Edwards, a psychologist educated at Stanford and UCLA, taught a seminar by the same name at the University of Southern California. She teamed up with Hoover, an established writer and columnist for *Life* and *Cosmopolitan*, to help singles navigate a world built for two.

A fellow bachelor thoughtfully gifted me the book early in the *Solo* project. The book opens with a sentiment that resonated with me: "If you are one of the 43 million singles in this country, you are undoubtedly-and-painfully aware of the considerable difficulties of being happily single in a society where being paired is widely regarded as the only natural, sane, healthy, and proper way to be."

I thought, *Forty-three million singles? There are three times as many singles as that in the United States. How old is this book?*

A swift glance at the publication page answered my question: 1974. Fifty years before this book you now hold in your hands, Edwards and Hoover were tackling many of the same topics—most notably, how to live alone, go out alone, and build friendships.

I had just started the *Solo* podcast and was eager to change the world. I could not help but think how fifty years from the publication of that book, the world felt stuck in the same place. I thought, *Fifty years from now, will someone hear my message and think the same thing?*

No. The world has changed more than demographically since 1974. Perspectives have changed dramatically, as demonstrated by the Solo Love Letters. People are looking past challenges to the opportunities of single living.

## THE SOLO'S PROMISE

I like to ask my students and podcast listeners, "Are you the hero in the story of your life?"

It is a provocative question, especially if you are familiar with the narrative structure of the hero's journey from Joseph Campbell's book *The Hero with a Thousand Faces*, which presents the narrative structure of the hero's journey. This ubiquitous narrative plays out in popular books and films, such as *The Matrix, Lion King,* and *The Odyssey.*

Luke Skywalker's saga in *Star Wars* is the quintessential hero's journey, which unfolds in three phases. First, the hero is called to an adventure outside of their world. Triggered by a call for help from Princess Leia, Luke departs from his dull-yet-familiar home on Tatooine in a spaceship. Next, the hero battles both external enemies and internal demons. Luke evolves from a whiney farm boy to a warrior with a strong moral compass. Vanquishing the enemy and changing as a person, the hero then returns triumphant. Spiritually and psychologically transformed as a Jedi Knight, Luke leads the rebel alliance to victory.

Indeed, the hero's journey is a real crowd-pleaser.

Because Solos make such good superheroes (and rebels), the hero's journey would seem to be an apt metaphor for a single to

Solo reinvention. However, there is another narrative arc—one that doesn't require you to leave the house to go Solo and change the world.

Kim Hudson discovered that many familiar stories fail to fit the hero's journey structure, including *Legally Blonde, Billy Elliot, Bend it Like Beckham,* and *Pride and Prejudice.* In this alternative narrative structure, which she calls the Virgin's Promise, protagonists are pressured to conform in the ordinary world— domesticated and struggling to express their true self. An unexpected opportunity leads them to a secret world, where they can be their authentic self. Their newfound authenticity threatens the status quo of their old world, unsettling the established order and causing chaos. The protagonist retreats—often alone—to reflect and decide whether to commit to this new path. After choosing their light and embracing this new identity, the protagonist reenters the ordinary world, which bends and brightens in response.

The Disney princess movie *Frozen* exemplifies the Virgin's Promise narrative. The protagonist, Elsa, starts her journey in Arendelle's castle. Pressured by royal expectations, she conceals her magical power to create ice and snow. The turning point arrives at her coronation, where her abilities are unintentionally exposed. With her secret out, Elsa seizes her freedom, creating an isolated ice palace nearby where she can express her true self. She declares, "Yes, I'm alone, but I'm alone and free!"

Despite the ensuing conflicts and her kingdom being plunged into eternal winter, Elsa makes a crucial decision to embrace her powers and true self. This phase of her journey sees her alone in her ice palace, grappling with the disruption her transformation has caused. Elsa "chooses her light" when she learns to control her powers with love instead of fear. Armed with this realization, Elsa re-enters with the kingdom, and her acceptance of her unique abilities triggers a profound transformation in the kingdom, ultimately making life better for everyone.

I hope this book can serve as your secret world—your ice palace of sorts.

I began with the thesis that singlehood is not as bad—and marriage is not as good—as you've been led to believe. Through examples of remarkable singles and scientific research, I hope I succeeded in making my case.

My desire, too, was for you to feel surrounded by people who understand your single life. I hope you will see your own experiences reflected in the Solo Love Letters. I smiled, nodded, fist pumped, and cried as I read the submissions. I was moved by the writers' camaraderie and vulnerability. If you felt adrift—feeling like you were "the only one"—I hope that is no longer the case.

Finally, I wanted you to recognize the opportunities of single living by adopting a Solo mindset. "Wholeheartedness" manifests by recognizing, accepting, and celebrating your singularity. Solos are unique, yet connected to a broader world. Neither less than nor liminal. "To parent oneself" ushers in greater self-reliance to take advantage of the richness of life—single or not. "Unconventional thinkers" question the rules of the relationship escalator and beyond. By not defaulting into domesticated thinking, you are free to break the rules, politely so.

In a world built for two, Solos are comfortable with the state of their relationships. The *Just Mays* would welcome an escalator ride but are not waiting around hopelessly—and don't have to worry about getting their dress stuck in it. (I've just been waiting to make an escalator joke and this is the last chance.) They are living remarkably in the meantime. The *No Ways* break the rules by saying "No" to "The One," which opens a wide array of non-romantic and nonsexual connections. The spicy *New Ways* are picking from a Cheesecake Factory–sized menu of unconventional relationships. My hope is that all of these Solos will further enhance their relationships—romantic or otherwise—by using relationship design to cocreate their own rules and agreements.

At first blush, this book seems to be about single living, why to celebrate it, and how to position singularity as a fundamental human experience. That is partially true, but really, the book is about transcending relationship status. It's about flourishing through purpose, creativity, and positive emotions, all the while maintaining a strong connection with a wider community. Singles, given their inherent freedom, contribute significantly to the world by creating music and art, by building businesses or innovating, and by taking roles like supportive aunts and uncles.

Solos brighten the "kingdom."

## WELCOME TO THE MOVEMENT

Writing this book changed my life. I better see how I have been domesticated and how I have become more comfortable getting off leash. I am comfortable with my choice to join a movement that harkens back to the first person to resist an arranged marriage.

Like the narrative in the Virgin's Promise, the transformation from single to Solo has the power to change the world. When enough people do it, single living will be impossible to ignore. Society will start seeing single living as indistinguishable from married life. Moving from one to the other will be celebrated, not commiserated. Businesses will redesign the products and services they offer and improve how they communicate with singles. Policymakers and pastors who have been focused on families will seek solutions to single people's problems. Academics will do more research that reveals the richness of going Solo.

Until then, welcome to the movement. No, I don't expect rallies or marches on Washington, DC. (Okay, maybe for you organizers—go ahead and march!) We will be revolutionaries and rebels simply by living remarkably. Like Susan B. Anthony, Marjorie Hillis, Henry Rollins, DTLA Josh, and Thelma, you will serve as a model to inspire others to break the rules in a world built for two. Maybe even Aunt Sally will be moved by the movement.

With that, I'll ask one last time: What are you waiting for?

Join the Solo community at
https://petermcgraw.org/solo/.

# ACKNOWLEDGMENTS

**M**y plan was to write this book and then find a publisher. Man plans. God laughs.

I got talked into writing a book proposal, and my literary agent, Jim Levine, pitched it to publishers. Everyone passed—except for one young, energetic editor, Elizabeth Gassman, who took a chance on a transgressive voice in a traditional body. Thank you, Liz!

I needed a lot of editing help. I am grateful to Liz, who cut one out of three words from the first draft. (If only I knew in advance which words, I would have not written them in the first place.) Another group of smart, generous people helped me save Liz a lot of headaches: Kimberly Kessler and Brannan Sirratt, especially. Three friendly readers, Mary Dahm, Suzette Smith, and Mark Ferne gave great notes and invaluable editorial suggestions. Laura Grant and Jessalyn Dean stepped up to help with a couple of chapters and figures. Kriss Rita was essential in curating and editing Solo Love Letters. Shane Mauss and Jennifer O'Donnell provided much-needed punch-ups.

Gratitude is like love. It should be given generously. Thank you, all.

The *Solo* podcast has been my laboratory and playground to develop many of the ideas presented here. I thank all my guests. I want to highlight some who were especially important to this endeavor: Julie Nirvelli, Kym Terrible, Iris Schneider, Amy Gahran, Laura Grant, Shane Mauss, Sasha Cagen, Kris Marsh, Kriss Rita, Suzette Smith, Monique Murad, Jessalyn Dean, and Mary Dahm. A tip of the Stetson to the podcast's design team— Mariah Baerend, Steffen Baerend, and Josh Mishell—and editor, James Martin. Thanks to those who provided media help, social and otherwise: Sophia Schelle, Veronica Welch, Erik Jefferies, and Nicole Mueksch.

Invaluable contributions came from my research team: Anant Gupta, Sarah Garcia, Daniel Lastine, Jorge Renteria, and especially Jenyfer Lara-Serrano. I also want to single out some scholars whose original research or advice was critical to the book: Bella DePaulo, Amy Gahran, Bill Von Hippel, Elyakim Kislev, Craig Wynne, Eric Klinenberg, Geoff MacDonald, Stephanie Coontz, Richard Meadows, Kris Marsh, Eli Finkel, Joseph Henrich, Caleb Warren, Michael Sargent, Jeff Larsen, Dan Bartels, Lawrence Williams, Ketaki Chowkhani, Kinneret Lahad, Iris Schneider, Chuan He, Nicole Reinholtz, Barb Mellers, Phil Tetlock, Danny Kahneman, and Shane Mauss. My gratitude extends to Larry Weissman and Sascha Alper, who encouraged me to better position my proposal, and Sheila Paxton who provided inspiration for naming the four types of singles.

An array of remarkable friends offered encouragement, advice, knowledge, and enthusiasm for the Solo project. I have love in my heart for them: Darwyn Metzger, Mary Dahm, Mark Ferne, Kym Terrible, Julie Nirvelli, Lawrence Williams, Stephen Morrison, Sheila Paxton, Todd Engmann, Rachel Beisel, James Craig, Janet Schwartz, Kathleen Vohs, Kristin Diehl, Jonathan Levav, Paul Shirley, Jessalyn Dean, Amy Gahran, Laura Grant, Paige Stephens, Joel Warner, Jeff Leitner, Ethan Decker, Kevin Monk, Eric Lassahn, Phil Fernbach, Matt De Caussin, Dan Cohen, Emma Chitters, Sarah Stinson, Christina Martinez, Bett

Morris, Meg Campbell, Barnet Kellman, Dan Ariely, David Yeats, Natalie Barandes, and Lacey.

To the Solo community (sign up at https://petermcgraw.org /solo/), your insight and stories have been essential. Special thanks to Jordan El-Hag, for pushing me to better define Solo in the early days of the podcast. Extra special thanks to the people who submitted Solo Love Letters. This book would not be the same without them.

A shout-out to three performance-enhancing places I spent a lot of time besides my apartment and office: The Process by Paul Shirley, Denver Sports Recovery, and countless cafés. Thanks also to the concierge in my "box in the sky" for helping with print jobs!

To my sister, Shannon, I love you.

If you flipped here wondering if you received much deserved thanks and failed to find your name, my apologies for the oversight. Your contribution mattered.

Onward!

# NOTES

## CHAPTER ONE

1. The term "animal husbandry" comes from the Middle English word "husbandry," which means the cultivation or management of household affairs. The word "husband" originally referred to a male head of a household or a farmer, who managed the resources of the household or farm.
2. Even today, the love marriage is not universally adopted. Arranged marriages are prevalent in many regions today, including but not limited to India, Pakistan, Bangladesh, Iran, Iraq, Afghanistan, Saudi Arabia, Oman, Yemen, the United Arab Emirates, Nigeria, Egypt, Sudan, Ethiopia, and Somalia.
3. The word "nuclear" had nothing to do with fusion or fission and everything to do with the atomization of the individual. The family structure became a small, self-contained unit, with parents and their children living together but separate from extended family.

## CHAPTER TWO

1. To be fair, this is not always a wholly beneficial choice. There are instances where a couple might be taxed at a higher rate. For example, if both spouses earn $50,000 per year, their combined income of $100,000 would place them in the 22 percent tax bracket. However, if they were both single and earned $50,000 each, they would each be in the 12 percent tax bracket, resulting in a lower overall tax bill.
2. Shout-out to Netflix, which offers employees a flat amount for healthcare regardless and lets employees without dependents can collect their unused portion in cash.

## CHAPTER THREE

1. The family has never made the trip to see Thelma.

2. There is an enjoyable irony here that the person who became a world expert on single living was able to do so because she had the ability to do whatever she wanted because she is single. Prior to her work on singlehood, Bella was a world-renowned researcher on lie detection. (Takeaway: People are not as good at detecting lies as they think they are.) I had applied to the PhD program at the University of Virginia and mentioned in my application that I had wanted to work with her. Small world that we came into each other's lives via singlehood!

## CHAPTER FOUR

1. While men are uniformly addressed as "Mr.," regardless of marital status, women were historically categorized as either "Miss" or "Mrs." based on their marital status. That began to change during the feminist movements of the 1960s and 1970s. The introduction of the neutral term "Ms." marked a significant change, largely due to the efforts of women's liberation activists who argued that women's titles shouldn't have to reveal their marital status, unlike men's. The launch of *Ms.* magazine in 1971, cofounded by Gloria Steinem and Dorothy Pitman Hughes, catapulted "Ms." into the mainstream.

2. I am so ultra-rational, I decided as a teenager that if I didn't drink, I couldn't have an alcohol problem. I was a teetotaler until I was twenty-five and have proudly returned to that lifestyle.

3. When I was younger and walking about the city I lived in, ever the planner, I would keep an eye out for places where I could sleep should I ever be homeless. One day, I realized that, should that ever happen, I was fortunate to have twenty couches (or even swanky guest rooms) of my friends that I could bounce between till I could get back on my feet.

## CHAPTER SIX

1. A group Solo trip involves a curated group of singles (and occasionally partnered people) traveling apart together. Participants may get their own rooms in a hotel, split an Airbnb, or stay in the same neighborhood. The trip is marked by huge swaths of free time, and one or two group activities a day—perhaps a museum trip or a group dinner. That way, one person can go to the gym (me), while

another sits in a café to read (also me), and someone else goes shopping (not me).

## CHAPTER SEVEN

1. Brandt took a hiatus from his hermitage for about ten years to study bookbinding, gaining worldwide recognition for his restoration work on historical books and ancient Bibles. He even restored a copy of John James Audubon's masterpiece, *Birds of America*. The one he restored from that series is now estimated to be worth $12.5 million—his family can't help but wonder why he didn't keep it.

## CHAPTER ELEVEN

1. Humans were built to walk—and walk a lot. Hunter-gatherers got somewhere between twelve thousand and twenty thousand steps a day. Experts say ten thousand steps is a good goal. The typical American walks less than five thousand steps. Solos, here's a motivating call-to-action: Aim for at least ten thousand steps as a way to maintain health and independence.

## CHAPTER TWELVE

1. Warner's view on romance is consistent with the *Just May* crowd: "Who knows what the universe will offer up with regard to a romantic relationship, but I am clear I am not putting my life on pause to figure that out. If you want to join me on my Solo journey, put out a thumb, show some hairy calf, and I will try and slow down long enough for you to jump aboard."

# SOURCES